Be a *Smart* mum Not a *Good* mum

5 Profound principles
to reclaim your mojo for a
satisfying and fulfilling family life

Nicky Tegg

Foreword by New York Times bestselling author Christy Whitman

BALBOA.PRESS

A DIVISION OF HAY HOUSE

Balboa Press books may be ordered through booksellers or by contacting:

Balboa Press
A Division of Hay House
1663 Liberty Drive
Bloomington, IN 47403
www.balboapress.com
844-682-1282

Because of the dynamic nature of the Internet, any web addresses or links contained in this book may have changed since publication and may no longer be valid. The views expressed in this work are solely those of the author and do not necessarily reflect the views of the publisher, and the publisher hereby disclaims any responsibility for them.

The author of this book does not dispense medical advice or prescribe the use of any technique as a form of treatment for physical, emotional, or medical problems without the advice of a physician, either directly or indirectly. The intent of the author is only to offer information of a general nature to help you in your quest for emotional and spiritual well-being. In the event you use any of the information in this book for yourself, which is your constitutional right, the author and the publisher assume no responsibility for your actions.

Cover Graphics/Art Credit: Claudia Rose Carter

Print information available on the last page.

ISBN: 978-1-9822-6071-2 (sc)
ISBN: 978-1-9822-6069-9 (hc)
ISBN: 978-1-9822-6070-5 (e)

Library of Congress Control Number: 2020925182

Balboa Press rev. date: 12/30/2020

I dedicate this book to my beautiful
daughters, Ashani and Jazmin.
If you choose to become a mum and you forget who you are,
this book will remind you.
Yours truly with love, mum xoxo

Contents

Acknowledgments

First and foremost, I wish to express an abundance of thanks and appreciation to my wonderful daughter Ashani for being my greatest teacher. Thank you for showing me how to love unconditionally, to forgive easily and to dream like a child again. I love you.

I would like to acknowledge with profound gratitude my soul mate, my best friend and my love, Nick. Thank you for supporting me in all of my dreams and visions even if they can be so crazy! Thank you for being my safe space and for never letting me give up. I believe in you just as much as you believe in me. I love you.

To all my teachers, Christy Whitman, Dr Shefali Tsabary, Shakti Gawain, Dr Wayne Dyer, Louise Hay, Abraham Hicks, Natalie Ledwell, Marci Shimoff, Sonia Ricotti, Lisa Nichols, Deepak Chopra, Eckhart Tolle, Don Miguel Ruiz, Gabrielle Bernstein, Sanaya Roman and Duane Packer, Jay Shetty, David R. Hamilton, Vishen Lakhiani, Joe Dispenza, Dimple Thakrar, Tony Robbins, I thank you and appreciate each and every one of you.

A special heartfelt thank you to Christy Whitman for teaching me the skills needed and for qualifying me as a life coach through the worlds best life coaching academy, Quantum Success Coaching Academy. Your continued support, belief in me, showing me what is possible will stay with me forever. I appreciate you.

A huge thank you to David Robert Ord for your genius editing skills and for adding the magic to this book. Thank you for believing in me, encouraging me, and for showing me the confidence I needed in my writing. I appreciate you.

I want to acknowledge my clients, past present and future. I wouldn't be doing what I do if it wasn't for you. Thank you for trusting me, co-creating with me, for your love and appreciation, and for showing up in my world. I appreciate you.

Last but not least, thank you to the one hundred women for allowing me to interview you as part of the research carried out for this book. I appreciate your time, honesty and the cups of tea! I appreciate you.

Be a Smart Mum,
Not a Good Mum
Foreword by Christy Whitman

Be a Smart Mum, Not a Good Mum offers an honest and insightful exploration into the unique personal challenges that women face as they evolve through the journey of motherhood. At the root of all these challenges is the loss of what author Nicky Tegg calls our "mojo," which is connection to the universal stream of energy that sources our creativity, vitality and zest for life. *Smart Mum* guides readers through five powerful principles for reclaiming their personal mojo – Source, Mindset, Action, Respond, and Trust – and provides dozens of interactive processes to help anchor these principles in our daily lives.

I met Nicky Tegg in 2015, as a student in my Quantum Success Coaching Academy. Nicky went on to become a certified Law of Attraction coach, and has participated in just about every course that I've offered since. The personal triumphs she recounts throughout this book are the result of Nicky wholeheartedly applying everything she has learned toward creating the life she envisioned for herself – even right down to the detail of the "Hay House" name which appears on the title page of this book.

At its core, *Be a Smart Mum, Not a Good Mum* is about accepting personal responsibility for nurturing our connection with the divine energy that sources us. Throughout these pages, you'll find practical strategies and techniques for holding on to your mojo and generating your own high-flying vibration, regardless of what anyone else is doing. Only when the connection within ourselves is rock-solid can we be the visionaries we desire to be, for our families, for our communities, and for the world.

Christy Whitman
New York Times bestselling author
Scottsdale, Arizona

Introduction

'She's better off without me.' My daughter Ashani was not even one, yet I was sinking fast into a state of powerlessness, with every notion of self-belief drowning. What was happening to me?

Images flashed through my mind of leaving my family and running away. But when I thought of not being with Ashani, my whole body went weak. A feeling of guilt, emptiness, and sadness rushed through every cell in my body.

'Everyone else seems to be living their happy-ever-after,' I told myself. 'Why not me? What is wrong with me? Why is everyone so horrible to me?'

I told myself, 'I can't do this anymore. I can't do *life* anymore.'

The pain was intense. I felt like my whole being was shutting down. I wondered, how can I live life feeling such emotional agony?

Having my own family was all I ever dreamt of from when I was a child. I always felt that I was meant to be happy. I imagined being a secure, confident, and present mum, married to a kind, loving, and fun man who adored me and our children. I thought of myself as healthy, fit, full of energy, and active. I would be a stay-at-home mum, running my own business from home and having fun with my family.

I envisioned us living in a cosy home with a large garden for our children to run around in. We went on family holidays and enjoyed life. This vision of living a satisfying and fulfilling family life was all I ever wanted.

I didn't understand why I wasn't happy. I married a good man and had a beautiful daughter. I had my own family. So why wasn't I happy and living my happily ever after? What had happened to the calm, fun, and joyful mum, and wife I was meant to be? Why were powerless thoughts stuck in my mind, like an endless loop? Why was I dissatisfied and unfulfilled?

Growing up, I was told that if I worked hard and was a good person, I would live happily ever after. I felt life had totally let me down.

I wanted my 'happy ever after' life so much that I desperately searched for it for decades, though in all the wrong places. I went to school and tried to get good grades. I attended university in search of a degree. I tried to be as kind, respectful, and giving to everyone. At work, I tried my best to be there every day, working as hard as I could. I did my best to make my man happy and be a good wife to him. I was determined to be a good mum for Ashani. I wanted our home to be a haven filled with love.

Instead, Ashani was playing by herself on the floor in our living room. Every few minutes, she looked at me with sad eyes. She longed for her mummy to hold her. It had been a week of no cuddles. I could see her, but something had taken over in me. All I could do was stare zombie like into space. I had nothing left to give. All the household chores were being attended to by my husband.

'Babe, in all the years I've known you, I've never seen you like this.' My husband looked into my eyes. 'It's like your light is gone.'

For a reason I cannot explain, I was suddenly jolted into awareness. Something inside me woke up. 'My light has gone,' I told myself. I could not believe it. The one thing I swore to myself that I would not do was to switch off my inner light.

I had never moved off my sofa so fast in my life. I went straight over to my beautiful daughter, picked her up, and held her tight. Looking into her eyes, I promised, 'Mummy will never be a victim ever again!'

It was October 2014, when I started my life over again—but this time on *my* terms. I decided that I was going to get to the bottom of finding my 'happy ever after.' I needed my mojo back!

I was sick and tired of trying to be this so-called good person that society had brainwashed me to be, promising all kinds of rewards for being good. Enough was enough. There had to be more than this to life. I decided to get smart.

The amazing, wonderful universe felt my intention and has supported it ever since. The power of life came rushing through me, to me, and from me. While Ashani was sleeping, I spent every evening for the next few years learning about myself, my mind, and how to live a fulfilling life. Hour after hour, I read self-development books, listened to audios, and researched how the mind works. I was awake until the early hours of every morning. I was on a mission not only to find my mojo, but to understand how I lost it.

When I sprang into action, I transformed every area of my life from lack to abundance, and from pain to joy. Even my body changed, as I dropped from a size 18 to a size 10. I found my dream job. I became a magnet, drawing to myself amazing people. Love, success, and happiness poured into my life. As my mojo returned, no area of my life was unaffected.

More importantly, I was no longer hijacked by the powerlessness that kept me from being present with Ashani. I learnt how to shift from the powerless feelings to powerful feelings and have been a present mum ever since.

I was trying to be a good mum because I did not feel good enough. But when I learnt to become a smart mum, I felt empowered, good enough, and worthy of living a satisfying and fulfilling family life.

It was then that I realised I could not keep what I had learned to myself. I had to share this with every woman in the world who was going through what I had endured.

I have made this book a quick and easy read because I know how busy us mums can be. The processes I will share with you are the processes I applied and still apply daily to connect to my mojo so I can live a satisfying and fulfilling family life.

If you engage in one process each day, you will see change in your life and a shift in how you feel. If you have lost your mojo, then living by the five principles and practicing the processes will help you find it again.

The biggest benefit you will receive from living these smart principles and applying the processes are shifting from disempowering emotions to empowering emotions. I like to call them mojo vibes or mojo-less vibes.

On the following pages you will find two bubble diagrams, mojo vibes and mojo-less vibes. As you apply the five principles to your everyday life and practice the processes, you will find that you experience more of the mojo vibes and less of the mojo-less vibes.

Another benefit is you will notice that your mojo vibes are contagious. Your children will feel safe and thrive off your vibes.

They will watch and learn how to connect to their own mojo should society teach them to disconnect to it. In my opinion, there is no better benefit that that.

I want to take a moment and really appreciate you for reading this book and allowing me to share my story with you. I am so deeply grateful to you for being another woman on this planet who is willing to find joy and to spread your light. The world needs your light to shine brightly. Thank you for showing up and having the drive to take charge of your life on *your* terms. On the other side of powerless is immense power—and that my friend is the key to the 'happy ever after' that feels so good, you will never look back.

Take a moment and have a look at the following mojo bubbles. Be honest with yourself and see which vibes you feel often.

You might be shocked at how many mojo-less vibes you feel, but please do not be disheartened. The first step to any kind of self-development, healing, and transformation is simply acknowledging how you are feeling.

Now, pick the vibes you would love to feel most of the time. As you go through this book, keep in mind of how you want to feel.

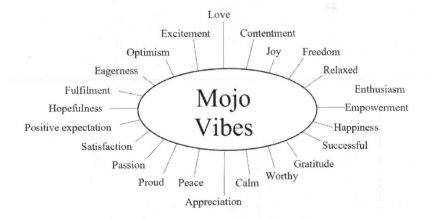

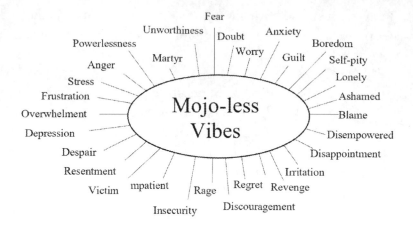

Being in a committed relationship can bring a lot of growth. Being a mother trebles the potential for growth. It introduces us to a whole *other* level.

Chapter One

S is for Source

Principle #1

You Are the Source of Your Health, Wealth, Joy, and Mojo

You are the source of your health, wealth, joy, and mojo. Not your children, your spouse, or even your parents.

This is the good news. If you are responsible for everything in your life, whether it is good or not, you can *change* it.

Do you want to hear the bad news?

The bad news is that you cannot blame anyone else for the state your life is in. You are responsible for the food, exercise, and sleep with which you tend your body. You are responsible for how much wealth you desire in your life. You are responsible for the amount of joy you would like to feel every day. You cannot blame your education, the economy, or your parents. It is not your child's fault that you have lost your mojo. Nobody and nothing have power over you unless *you* give them that power.

You alone are also responsible for your mojo. Say it out loud: 'I am the source of my health, wealth, joy, and mojo.'

How does it feel when you say this? Can you own your responsibility, knowing that your life will only get better because *you* are now in charge?

When I realised that I was responsible for how I felt, I came alive. It began to dawn on me that I am more than flesh and bones. I am so much more than just my physical being. I am a powerful being living a physical life.

I refer to this powerful being as my 'essence.' Sometimes I speak of it as a *divine* aspect of myself. It is the non-physical part of me that breathes and experiences my physical life through my material makeup. It is this *essence* that has desires and seeks to be a creative individual.

Let me be clear with what I have in mind when I speak of our 'essence.' One afternoon, a student was walking home from school. His thoughts were wandering, when suddenly his name, 'Jerry,' said itself in his mind. Stopping in his tracks, he whispered to himself, 'I am.'

This revelation was astonishing. 'I exist,' he realised as he started to walk again. He was fourteen years old.

As he thought about this experience, he realised that *everything he understood to be himself was not who he really was.*

In his adult years, the boy in question became a professor. One day a student asked a question in class. As the professor launched into his answer, he said, 'I caught a glimpse of his eyes. I was stunned. My God, there was a person in those eyes. And I was not speaking to that person, or to any person.'

Our essence is often referred to as our spirit or soul. It is the core of our being. This is the aspect of us that enjoys perfect health, has unbounded joy, is abundantly wealthy, and harbours our *mojo*.

The human tendency to 'look at ourselves' is captured in the expressions we commonly use to refer to ourselves, such as our self-image, self-worth, and self-esteem. These usually involve presenting a front to the world, which is quite different from being *authentic*, so that everything we say and do is *genuine*.

Most think of their *ego* as who they are. But today, more and more of us are realising that our ego—the part of us that majors in our self-image—is not who we really are at all. It's a construct of the mind. We grow up seeing ourselves a certain way, then we spend our lives trying to have others validate the way we see ourselves.

When this fails, we go through an identity crisis. That is what was happening to me.

Our ego is about feeling valid in our own eyes and in the eyes of the world around us. Ironically, were we truly convinced of our validity, there would never be a need to feel we have to convince others. Without in any way suggesting that we dismiss others or are rude to them, the fact is that were we true to ourselves in every way, it would not overly concern us what anyone else thinks of us.

This authentic essence, which is the core of our being, is what I have in mind when I speak of our *mojo*. Our essence is an aspect of us that is powerful—a positive energy that pulsates through us, to us, and from us.

Life is an inside out job. Our health, wealth, and joy emanate from within us. I had been so busy chasing love, health, wealth, and happiness *externally*, which is why I eventually crashed. As my ego plummeted to earth, I felt disconnected from just about every aspect of my life, even my young daughter. No amount of money I earned was ever enough. No amount of love could satisfy me. Despite all the people and possessions that surrounded me, I felt empty and alone.

It was when I connected with my essence—that pure, powerful. positive energy that was my core self—that I at last became that happy, secure, and present mum I dreamt of being. This is when I developed a co-creating relationship between my divine center and my everyday life.

When we connect to our essence, we experience a sense of wellbeing that surpasses anything people have in mind when they speak of "happiness." This involves a joy that is not linked to whatever may be happening in our external world. Unlike happiness, which is always fleeting, this joy is enduring. When we connect to our essence, we feel the joy that is *inherent* in who we are, but that for much of our lives has been occluded. This joy is long lasting because our essence is the source of our inner light—our *mojo*.

You are the source of your power. It is up to you to connect with your inner wellspring of health, wealth, joy, and mojo. It is not the responsibility of anyone to do this for you. Once you connect with your source, you will find that any emptiness or loneliness you may have been feeling simply vanishes.

As I will show you, one of the best ways I know to connect with our essence is through sitting in stillness. When we still our mind from all the constant chatter it tends to engage in, a calm descends on us. We can accomplish this simply by sitting and watching our thoughts for just a few minutes each day.

We have been so conditioned to believe that happiness comes from the outside. If we work hard, people assure us, we will receive life's 'goodies.' But what good is it to having these goodies if we are feeling empty and disconnected inside of ourselves?

I am in my forties and I feel healthier now than I did in my twenties. I feel wealthier now than I did when I worked my bones off. I feel more joy now than I did when I was young and had no responsibilities. All this happened to me when I went to my source and built a relationship with my inner being.

When the non-physical aspect of ourselves and our physical being connect, magic happens. We discover we have all sorts of inner resources. These inner resources are the tools we use when we create our life *from the inside out*. These tools include our thoughts, emotions, imagination, focus, and the choices we make. These inner resources spring from our essence, enabling us to create the health we want, the wealth we want, and the joy we want.

When we use our inbuilt resources the right way, the universe supports us. We no longer need to stress, struggle, or suffer in order to thrive in the physical world.

In reality, I never lost my mojo. It was with me all along, but I could not connect with it. This is the case with many of us, since most of us lose touch with much of our inner being in childhood—if not *all* of who we truly are.

The day I promised my daughter Ashani that her mummy would never be a victim again, I took back all my power. Taking back 100% responsibility for my life put me in touch with my health, wealth, joy, and mojo.

I decided that I, not someone else, was going to be the source of my happiness. I let everyone off the hook. It was no longer their job to make me happy. I stopped needing things from others, including my husband. I took the burden of making myself joyous from him and decided that I was in charge of my joy.

When I started this journey, I didn't have much money at all. In fact, I had £2 to my name. I felt lonely and empty, and I was unhappy in my marriage. I was overweight. My friends were not making any effort with me. But after saying 'no more, enough is enough,' and taking total responsibility, my energy shifted from victim to victor.

When you make this shift within yourself, everything changes. You feel better, lighter, and in charge of your destiny. Then comes the external evidence of your new energy, often in the form of small gifts. I think of these as gifts from the universe.

In the first year of going within, taking responsibility for my feelings and my experiences, I witnessed many changes in myself and my family. My daughter reflected my positive vibe and mirrored my connection with myself. She became calmer, happier, content.

If you look at your external life, are you satisfied? When you look in the mirror, do you feel complete? When you look at your bank balance, are you happy? When you look at your relationships with your family, friends, and co-workers, does it feel like everything is going well?

If you answered 'no' to any of these aspects of your everyday life, I invite you to study the following processes and apply them to your everyday life.

Process #1

The Essence of Your Mojo

Your mojo affects your vibe, your demeanour, your self-esteem. But this isn't the sort of self-esteem you have to *talk* yourself into. It is a deep sense of your value, and *it springs from within*.

We have all been around someone from whom we felt either a good vibe or a bad vibe. Children instantly sense a person's vibe, especially little babies since they are closely connected to their essence—until the world around them causes them to lose sight of their inner power. Incidentally, this is why I never make my daughter go to anyone she does not gravitate toward. I trust her sense, her intuition.

Our vibe is the energy others feel when they are around us. A *mojo-less* vibe is the mark of someone whose energy revolves around resentment, blame, and stress. A person with a *mojo* vibe is someone who experiences energy that arises from deep within them in the form of love, joy, optimism, excitement, and a sense of contentment.

You can feel someone's vibe when you are in the same vicinity as them. It does not matter how much someone tries to hide it with a smile and says they are 'fine', you nevertheless feel their vibe because it is an energy that doesn't lie.

Mojo-less vibes attract people who themselves give out mojo-less vibes. A person with a positive demeanour is a person who thinks positive thoughts and has a positive attitude toward themselves, others, and life in general—not because they try to think positively, but because they are tuned into a part of themselves where such a demeanour arises *spontaneously* within them.

Someone with a positive attitude toward life—the kind of positivity that springs from their core being—rarely ever thinks powerless thoughts or feels powerless emotions. They are more solution-focused than problem-focused.

They don't see problems, only challenges. Such are viewed as opportunities for growth.

A healthy self-esteem emanates from a person who has a healthy sense of themselves. They don't 'believe' they are worthy, they *know* they are. Instead of hoping to be 'good enough,' whether they satisfy the whims of others is never an issue. Self-esteem arises naturally from their *essence*.

Someone with a healthy self-esteem instinctively says kind things to themselves, praises themselves, compliments themselves. They are always loving toward themselves, proud of themselves, and believe that they belong in the world. They are their own cheerleader.

I am not talking about an egotistic, narcissistic form of self-esteem. When we see ourselves through the eyes of our essence, we attract desirable opportunities to ourselves. A person with a positive demeanour attracts life-giving friendships and relationships. People with a healthy self-esteem are emotionally intelligent, encouraging, supportive, and believe in the other person's potential. This is the essence of one's mojo.

The key is to live a satisfying and fulfilling life on *your* terms, not those of someone else.

I encourage you to spend a day pondering the following questions while you are cooking, doing the laundry, on the school run, travelling to your place of work, in the shower, brushing your teeth, or during a tea break. The longer your mind is searching its database, which is your subconscious, for the answers, the more your mind will be imprinted with a new way of thinking that will spontaneously bring you joy.

EXERCISE

For quicker results, write down the answers to the questions below. Pen and paper are the first steps to creation. However, if you have been feeling like a mojo-less bubble for some time, a simple task of finding a pen could feel like a chore! (I get it. That was me.)

1) Which people in your life and activities give you positive feelings?

Example: My family, my best friend, and my life coach. Swimming, writing, reading self-help books, comedies, socialising, fresh air, and uplifting music. (Refer to the mojo vibe bubble diagram to see which good feelings you feel, on page xix.)

2) Which areas of your life do you think positive thoughts about?

Example: Relationships, health, career, finance, social or anything more personal to you.

3) What qualities and attitudes do you like about yourself?

  Example: Organised, easy going, sense of humour, ambitious, focused, can do attitude, solution focused, generous.

Check in with yourself. How do you feel after answering these questions? Acknowledging how you are feeling is so much more empowering than when someone else acknowledges you. Even the slightest shift in your vibe is mirrored in your mojo.

Process #2

Claim Back Your Mojo!

When you make a declaration with a burning intention, the universe supports you all the way. I am not just passing on to you something I read in a book. I am speaking from first-hand experience.

When I declared to my daughter that her mummy would never again be a victim, I friggin meant it with every cell in my body. I was making a declaration to the universe with every intention never to fall victim to anyone or anything again. The entire universe supported me by bringing me ideas, insights, the right people, the right resources, and the circumstances that would help me to reclaim my unique path.

It does not matter who or what you gave your mojo away to. Focus only on claiming it back. If you are hung up on past hurts or undesirable experiences, you alone are responsible for shortening or lengthening the bridge between where you are and creating a life you love.

You can make yourself a promise if you like: "I will never give my mojo away to anyone or anything ever again."

Your mojo belongs to you and is uniquely yours. It makes you who you are. It's the fuel you need to create a life you love. Declare to the universe that you claim back your mojo, and do so with intention, as if you really mean it.

When you feel conviction, you will not stop until you get your mojo back, no matter how long it has been missing—even if that's your earliest days on the planet. There is no room for negotiation. It is not up for discussion. Your words are fuelled with feeling, which causes the universe to figure that you are serious, since energy listens to energy. If your energy is not moving when you make your declaration, the universe cannot hear you.

EXERCISE

1) Start by getting that energy moving in your body. Jump up and down. Run around. Do star jumps. Do whatever you need to do to move your body and shift your energy. If you do not feel your energy rise, keep moving your body.

2) Declare out loud with conviction until your cells vibrate, "I claim back every ounce of my mojo."

3) Spend the day affirming your declaration. As you go about your day, stop every now and then and affirm, "I claim back every ounce of my mojo." Say it a hundred times. Tweak the words to suit your personal energy, as long as it feels like you are expressing a burning intention to claim back your mojo

Again, for faster results, write it down. Write it down a hundred times. The more you write it down, the more the vibe rises and the quicker the universe gets to work for you.

I used to say, 'If you want something, go get it.' Now
I say, 'If you want something, *write it down.*'

Process #3

Forgiveness

Whenever I heard the word 'forgiveness,' it felt so big that I would cringe. My stomach knotted up from the resistance I had to forgiving those I felt had stolen my light, my power, my mojo.

'Why should I forgive them?' I told myself. 'They don't deserve to be forgiven after betraying me, hurting me, and breaking me down to rock bottom.' I felt angry at the way I had been treated by people in my life who I believed ought to love and support me, especially after I married and had a child.

Do you relate? Do you feel betrayed and hurt by individuals in your life?

Every time I thought about forgiveness, all the painful memories flooded my consciousness. I would count all the times I was treated badly. Forgiving the perpetrators felt like letting them off the hook. I did not want to let them off the hook! I wanted them to own up to being wrong and ask for my forgiveness.

Blaming others for my feelings was so much easier than forgiving them. Blame is always easier than taking responsibility. Believe me, to take responsibility for how you feel, your life experiences and how you are treated, takes guts.

Blaming others is a cop out.

It is a coward's game to blame others, and you are not a coward. How do I know this? Because it takes pluck to do the inner work you have chosen to do. It takes stick-to-itiveness to read a book like this and stay with the process. You need gumption to make real changes in your life. To be the woman you want to be is a tall but doable task.

Forgiveness means letting go of emotional pain. Holding onto hurt stops us from creating a satisfying and fulfilling family life. There is no transformation in a life in which we hold onto pain. We only store up more hurt for the future. The resistance involved spills into the various areas of our life, affecting our health, relationships, finances, career, and the atmosphere in our home.

When mum is happy, the family is happy. When mum is unhappy, the family is unhappy. There is a ripple effect. When we hold onto hurt, we unconsciously hurt others, especially those we love. When I am full of joy, my daughter Ashani thrives off my vibe. When I am feeling in love with life and empowered, my husband Nick is so much happier.

Being a happier mum makes forgiving and letting go of emotional pain worth every bit of discomfort. Going from a victim's 'poor me' stories to a life filled with abundance, health, wealth, and joy is so worthwhile.

Forgiving may not be the easiest thing to do. But speaking from experience, it is one of the most rewarding. Letting go of the pain someone has caused does not mean we automatically become friends again, unless this is our wish. Neither does forgiveness mean we agree with what someone has done. To forgive does not make the behaviour okay. We can forgive, let go of the pain, and release the person from our life if that is what we choose. If, due to family attachments, we cannot release the person from our life, we can release ourselves energetically and emotionally. We can then create healthy boundaries so that we no longer need them on an emotional level.

Forgiving is for *us*. We are doing it for our own benefit, not for the person who wronged us. We do not even have to tell the person that we have forgiven them, since it isn't important that they know.

When someone hurts another person, it is because the individual is themselves hurt. No one can share with another what they themselves lack. For some, the lack manifests in being unloving, failing to show empathy and compassion, or being disrespectful.

If you try to obtain understanding and emotional support from an emotionally immature person, you set yourself up to experience disappointment. If you seek respect from someone who does not respect themselves, once again you set yourself up. If someone is thoughtless, inconsiderate, unhelpful, or uncaring, do not expect them to be able to meet your needs. When they cannot, don't take it personally. It is their choice to show up in the world the way they choose to show up.

It is not your responsibility to dictate how others behave. If someone in your life chooses to be critical, judgmental, and unresponsive, it is their choice. You are not responsible for how someone shows up. You are only responsible for how *you* choose to show up. Resenting someone for not giving you what they simply do not have hurts only yourself, not them. Blaming others for not giving you what you could not give yourself is a recipe for failure. As we saw in Principle 1, "*You* are the source of your health, wealth, joy and mojo."

Notice I did not say your spouse is the source of your health, wealth, joy, and mojo. Neither are your parents the source of your health, wealth, joy, and mojo—and that includes your mother-in-law.

When you give yourself the credit for building the best life you can build for yourself, it's empowering. People will treat you the way you teach them to treat you. I found this difficult to digest, given that I had taught people to take advantage of me. I had encouraged people to depend on me day and night, which allowed them to walk all over me, disrespecting me and belittling me. People thought they could criticise me, control me, manipulate me.

How did I teach people to treat me this way? Instead of saying 'no' when I did not wish to do something, I instead said 'yes.' I lacked the courage to stand up for myself. I had no idea that if someone didn't like my 'no,' I could remove myself from them.

I didn't want to offend anyone, let alone upset them. Because I lacked a solid sense of myself, I wanted people to see me as someone who never falls, never gets exhausted. I sought to be a person who is hard core and never gets upset by others. I wanted everyone to think that nothing bothered me. Perhaps you resonate with this?

The entire way I presented myself gave others a false impression of who I really am. When someone criticised me or belittled me, I simply laughed it off. They didn't see the resentment that built up in me. In fact, no matter how hurt I felt, I allowed them to continue wasting my energy and time. I would even spend money on them. No wonder they thought it was just fine to criticise me.

I could easily have said, 'I won't allow you to speak to me that way.' Instead, I permitted them to cross the line, ignoring any boundaries I might set. Everyone knew that my boundaries meant nothing.

Forgiveness involves letting go of our past experience with someone. We have to let events of the past that we cannot change pass out of our lives. It means letting go of the old you and stepping into a stronger you, with the lessons that your past has taught you informing a different future.

The trick to this is that instead of seeing people as either friends or enemies, we see them as our teachers. The gift of this is the person we become as we step boldly into a future that honours our essential self.

When someone is being less than kind, instead of taking it personally, see it as the universe's way of teaching a valuable lesson. This enables us to take full responsibility for our feelings. As we acknowledge what we hoped to draw from them in the way of kindness, validation, reassurance, or understanding, we release them from the need to support us by giving these things to ourselves. In this way we take our power back, bringing our mojo back to life.

If you are ready to ditch all blame, the first step is to forgive yourself for not knowing better. Oprah's friend Maya Angelou taught her an important principle, which is that when we know better, we do better.

Forgive yourself for expecting others to meet your emotional needs. Forgive yourself for giving others the responsibility for your health, wealth, joy, and mojo. Forgive yourself for giving your power away.

Spend a day forgiving your past self for all the times you had anything less than kind thoughts toward anyone. Forgive yourself for all the times you were rude to someone or disrespectful to them, especially in the case of a past romantic partner. If you judged or criticised anyone, whether it was to their face or in the silence of your mind, forgive yourself. Whether someone deserved your criticism does not matter, as it's not our responsibility to teach people a lesson. Life will present them with their own lessons. If they wish to grow from such lessons or choose to stay stuck, this is their issue. They are having their own life experience, and you are having yours.

EXERCISE

I invite you to close your eyes as you imagine a past version of yourself standing in front of you. Look into her eyes and feel compassion for her. Greet her like you would your child, telling her she didn't know better in the past. You might say, "Hey sweetheart, you didn't know better back then, but that's okay. You know better now. I forgive you and I love you so much." Then hug her compassionately. This process is transforming because it releases you from the burden of guilt, regret, self-blame, and means you have no reason to beat yourself up. You go from judging yourself to loving yourself.

Spend the day forgiving others, one by one. Line them all up if you have a que of people like I did. Use the same process as you used for yourself, or you can change the words if you need to. If you cannot bring yourself to hug them just yet, that's okay. The purpose of this process is to set yourself free.

This is one of the hardest things to do, so acknowledge your courage. As you free yourself from chains of pain, your external life will increasingly reflect your inner freedom.

People look for financial freedom or freedom time wise. What they are really seeking is freedom from their pain. Once you feel complete inner freedom, you will find you stop chasing people and things to make you happy. Suddenly, they all appear when you least expect it.

Process #4

The Power of Meditation

There is so much power in meditation and the list of benefits is endless. People who meditate report greater clarity, focus, energy, and better health internally as well as externally. They also sleep more deeply, which keeps them looking youthful as it slows down the aging process. You become calmer, relaxed, and less bothered by things. You are happier, and you become more open to receiving life's goodies. Above all, the most important benefit of meditation is the connection you feel to your essence.

There are so many ways to meditate, including guided meditation, silent meditation, focused meditation—basically, anything that slows the mind down to a watching state can be considered meditation. When I sit quietly and immerse myself in a large jigsaw, my mind is in a meditative state. I find that instead of thinking thoughts, I'm focussing on the jigsaw.

Meditation is a way to recapture and enhance your mojo.

Researchers tell us that the human mind thinks on average 60,000 thoughts a day. We are only consciously aware of 2,000 of these thoughts. The rest of the 58,000 thoughts occupy our subconscious mind.

I was pretty horrified a few years ago when I had a good look at my life. My subconscious thoughts torpedoed my mojo, resulting in the powerlessness I experienced. This affected my mental, emotional, and physical health, as well as impacting my relationships, finances, and lack of a social life. Not only did my home feel like a prison, even my car was falling apart.

Entering a state of silence interjects a pause into the powerless thoughts that maraud our subconscious. With our thoughts paused, the negativity in our life also enjoys such a pause. When our negativity is paused, we become open to receive what we desire. Without all those powerless thoughts that on a day-by-day basis undermine our intentions, the negative vibes cease. We awaken to our mojo, which enables us to create the sort of life we relish.

To sit still and simply watch my thoughts is one of the best practices I have ever engaged in. This enables me to get me through all the challenges life throws at me. It is amazing how much positivity I can manifest in my life in just five to twenty minutes of daily meditation.

The most common excuse I hear from my clients is, 'I'm a busy mum, so I don't have time to meditate.' This is understandable, given that the mind goes straight into fear whenever a chance arises to be happy. Don't be shocked if your mind freaks out. You have allowed it to think thousands and thousands of thoughts all day long, so it's bound to resist the calm that arises from meditation, especially if you are new to this practice. Your ego will give you so many reasons not to meditate.

And the time factor? Every single person gets twenty-four hours each day, which is 1,440 minutes a day. Spending up to twenty minutes a day for yourself as you connect to the source of your health, wealth, joy, and mojo leaves you with another 1,420 minutes. Don't you think you can afford twenty minutes for yourself?

I find the best time to meditate is first thing in the morning and last thing at night. When my daughter was a toddler, I meditated fifteen minutes first thing in the morning before she awakened, then meditated twenty minutes during her lunchtime nap. I also found five to twenty minutes for myself before I went to bed. When I did this, I found that I was less frustrated and irritated. As I became calmer and more relaxed within myself, as well as among the people who occupied my day—especially with Ashani, who was a toddler at the time.

It can be so easy to be focussed on our external life. We look in the mirror and see the external shell of our body. We take a bath and are cleaning the external self. We look for love and immediately think of a person external to ourselves. We think of prosperity and immediately think of the physical aspect represented by money, which is external. Even if we think of joy, we picture an external experience such as a social event or a holiday abroad. We think of health and immediately think of exercise, as well as healthy foods and beverages. For many, when they think of God, they immediately think of an external being.

I am not suggesting that any of this is wrong. I absolutely believe that healthy food and beverages, exercise, money, holidays, socialising, and relationships enhance our experience of life. The quality and quantity of external elements in our lives are in fact a mirror of the quality and quantity of how much we spend connecting with our essence.

The benefits of meditation include:

Inner peace in the midst of drama

Improved concentration and focus

Activates creativity

Emotional balance

Calmness

Relaxed outlook to life

Less triggered by people

Reduced stress and anxiety

A better quality of life

Sound mental health

Slows down aging

More in the present and not worried about the past or future

Connection to intuition

Connection to the Devine, your essence.

How to meditate:

When people think of the term meditation, they automatically think of a Buddha in orange or white cloth reciting the mantra 'OM' repeatedly all day long in a lotus position.

Meditation is best performed sitting in a chair with your feet flat on the floor with your back straight. Or if you are comfortable you can sit in a lotus posture, however this is not necessary. Lying down to meditate is not recommended as you can fall asleep. Also meditating on a full stomach is not recommended either as you will feel sleepy.

Being in a meditative state, your sense of awareness is heightened yet you are fully alert and conscious. When we come out of meditation, we feel more peace with the world and more at home in our present life.

Meditating first thing in the morning when you wake up is the best time of the day as your subconscious is wide open. Setting your alarm twenty minutes earlier to meditate in the morning will be worth the positive and calm flow through your day.

Meditating on a mantra is powerful because whatever affirmation you are repeatedly reciting as a mantra while you are in a meditative state eventually becomes a subconscious belief.

When my daughter was in the toddler stage, I meditated on the mantra 'I am a calm and present mum.' Instead of feeling frustrated and occupied with thoughts about the situations or people that were upsetting me, my days flowed calmly, and I was present with Ashani. I will talk more about beliefs later in chapter two.

EXERCISE

Modify your meditation according to your level of experience with meditating.

Beginner: If you are an absolute beginner simply focus on your breath for a few minutes in the morning and before you go to bed. As the thoughts come in, simply allow them to pass without responding to them and without self-judgement. Then gently put your focus back on your breath.

Pro: If you are a pro at meditating, which you will be after practicing meditation every day for a while, silence your mind and connect to the stillness of your essence for twenty minutes. You will feel the pulsation of the energy flowing through you from within.

If you are seeking calm and peace in your day, meditate on the mantra 'I am calm and peaceful' for five to twenty minutes. You can change the mantra to anything you wish to feel.

1) Find a quiet and comfortable place to do your daily practice of meditation.

2) Sit up with a straight back and adjust your body until you are comfortable.

3) Close your eyes and begin with long and slow breaths in through your nose, filling up your stomach with air and then slowly releasing your breath through your mouth.

4) Continue your meditation choosing the level you wish to meditate at--beginner, pro, or use a mantra if you wish to direct your energy toward a particular feeling such as peace, calm, or relaxation.

5) Slowly bring your awareness back to your physical body. Gently open your eyes and go about your day with this wonderful feeling of peace.

Process #5

Hold onto Your Mojo!

Now that you are clear what your mojo is and have claimed it back, the next task is to work on fine-tuning it so you are ready to create a satisfying and fulfilling family life.

I used to give my mojo away at the drop of a hat. When I say, "give my mojo away," what I really mean is that I allowed people to trample on my truth to the extent that I couldn't hear my inner self, my essence, at all.

All kinds of situations and circumstances stood ready to receive it, from my daughter to my husband, family, friends, my finances, my body, and my environment in general. Now I hold onto my mojo about 90% of the time by not giving it away to anyone or anything external to me.

If I am faced with a challenging situation or a difficult person, I say silently in my mind, "Hold onto your power, Nicky. All is well. You are safe and protected."

When the brain detects fear, the body contracts, the breath becomes short and shallow. This is when we are prone to react irrationally. Before we know it, we get into a spiral and lose touch with our mojo.

It is up to you to decide what is more important to you in terms of your health, wealth, and joy. Or would you rather bank on getting people to be different, the weather to be nicer, your partner appreciating you, your mother-in-law asking after you when she calls her son, your children's room being tidier, or that extra bit of flab under your arm toned up?

When you witness what you can manifest just from holding onto your mojo, you won't let people and circumstances move in and get comfortable inside your mind. Your time and energy will become so much more valuable to you.

Hey, we are human. I still unconsciously give my power away to people and circumstances now and then. However, I may do this within the first ninety seconds, then I consciously take it back with the statement, 'Hold onto your power, Nicky. All is well. You are safe and protected.'

I am so much better at holding onto my power now than I was when I first started to practice this. When you make a conscious choice to hold onto your power, you may find that every person and situation you used to give your power away to suddenly presents themselves. If this happens, tell yourself, 'I can do this.' As you respond to people and situations in this new way, they will start to either change naturally or fall out of your life.

It is said that what we resist, persists. If you resist a person or situation, it will remain in your life and may even grow bigger. It is only when you stay centred, with your energy undisturbed, that change occurs. As you go through all the processes in this book, holding onto your power will become easier. You will be able to hold onto it longer and longer. Catching any resistance will become quicker. In no time at all, you will be a pro.

When my husband Nick is in a low mood, he becomes somewhat distant. He goes quiet and seems miserable. I used to give my mojo away by trying to get him to come out of his funk. I wasn't accepting of him as he was. It irked me to allow him to be miserable. A few years ago, after three weeks of enduring such a negative vibe, I told myself enough was enough. I could not take anymore. Losing my patience, I told him either to lighten up or get out of the house.

This led to him being even more miserable. One time this lasted three solid months. It was the time when I was first claiming my mojo back. He resisted my changes, and I resisted his resistance. One day I realised that the longer I resisted his low energy, the longer he was intent on staying in that energy.

Today, I can love him and hold onto my mojo whatever his mood. I have noticed that he's only down for a day or two, whereas before it used to be weeks, if not months. I had to choose my health, wealth, and joy over needing my husband to be more joyful. It was a hard choice at first because I figured I was being selfish by not caring about him. When I realised, I was only responsible for myself and my daughter Ashani, I stopped feeling guilty.

To show up as my best self, so that my daughter gets the best of me, meant choosing my mojo over my husband's happiness. I had to give the responsibility for his joy back to him. It was never my responsibility to make him happy. Thank goodness for that because it was really hard work. It is emotionally, mentally, and physically draining to make someone happy when they won't take responsibility for their own happiness.

I had to keep reminding myself that the source of my husband's health, wealth, and joy lay with him discovering that his mojo was readily available within himself. I had to love him enough to allow him to find and connect to his own essence.

The day I stopped giving my mojo away was a huge shift in my life and in our marriage. We are now closer than we have ever been. We now connect at a deeper level because we are both connected to our own essence first and foremost. Our relationship went from co-dependent to co-creating. No, it did not happen overnight. It required a gradual process, but it was worth every single bit of holding onto my power, regardless of how uncomfortable it felt to do so.

Most of the mothers I coach start off giving their power away to their spouse, and consequently they are stuck in blame. They resent their spouse. After practicing holding onto their power, their relationships slowly become happier and more deeply connected. They again find their partners attractive. That it takes two to tango is a myth. It only needs one person to make internal shifts that impact everyone else. Holding onto your mojo is worth every bit of discomfort you may at times feel.

Our mojo not only affects our relationship, but it also impacts our finances. Most people give their power away to their bank balance. I see people stressed and at times worried sick. Doubt and fear reign when it comes to their finances. Giving away their power to worry does nothing to change their bank balance. On the contrary, it makes the problem grow bigger.

At first when I only had £2 to my name, it was quite a job to hold onto my power. The weather was starting to turn, winter was fast approaching, and my daughter needed a warm coat. I could not buy her a winter coat with £2. It felt uncomfortable to say to myself,

"Hold onto your power. All is well. You are safe and protected." What I really wanted to do was complain and cry.

A parcel arrived from a family member with a winter coat. At first, I felt sad that it was not me who could buy my own daughter a winter coat. I had to hold onto my power and tell myself that I would buy my daughter's coat next winter. I chose to be grateful to the universe for giving a family member the idea of buying a winter coat. Within a month I had enough money to buy my daughter a second winter coat. This is how the universe works.

Had I spent my time and energy feeling the lack of money, envious of my wealthy family member, or sad that I could not even buy my own daughter a warm coat, I would have denied the source of my wealth the opportunity to create the very things I needed. I would also have denied myself the joy of my mojo.

Worse still, I would have denied my daughter the best version of her mummy. No way would I give my daughter the worst version of myself. And over a coat? By holding onto my power, I maintained my mojo and retained my powerful vibe, my positive demeanour, and my healthy self-esteem.

A hundred pounds came into my experience as a gift from my dad. For no reason, he just showed up at my home one day and said he had an urge to go to the bank and withdraw £100 and give it to me. He had no idea that I only had £2 to my name and my daughter needed a winter coat. I was grateful to the universe for planting the idea in his mind.

A few weeks later, it was my birthday. I received an abundance of money, a lot more than I had before. A couple of months later it was Christmas, and I received an abundance of money again. The more I practiced holding onto my mojo, the more life gave to me. As a result, my daughter, husband, and everyone else in my life benefited too. The more I received, the more I had to give. The more I gave, the more I received. It's a beautiful cycle of giving and receiving. The more you hold onto your power, the more joy you have. The more joy you feel, the more life gives you to be joyful about.

If people in your life zap your mojo, ask yourself what is more important to you? Do you want to be the blood for the energy vampire in terms of your health, wealth, and joy? Being the blood for the energy vampire is not going to bring you a satisfying and fulfilling family life.

I have removed myself from many people I once chose to give my power to. I had invited them into my house, knowing I would be left emotionally, mentally, and physically drained. I chose to visit these people. I chose to spend my precious time here on earth with those who zapped my power. It wasn't their fault. I taught them how to treat me by showing up as someone willing to give my power away. And for what? To feel accepted and loved. No thanks, baby!

I now love myself enough to say, 'no more.' I now love myself enough to remove myself from people who don't feed my inner being. At first, I felt quite alone. I noticed I was spending more and more time by myself. Yet somehow, I felt happy. I was in so much more joy on my own than I was when I was surrounded by others.

I had to learn not to give my power away to loneliness. Once I held onto my power during the times when tinges of loneliness crept in, I quickly shifted my vibe to gratefulness for the life-giving people who were on their way into my life. Within no time, they started to appear. Now that I can handle an abundance of life-giving people, I have a fantastic social life filled with incredible human beings.

It was worth every bit of discomfort when I was in transition. The gap between letting go of the old and expecting the new is the uncomfortable part. I transitioned from an overweight size 18 to a healthy size 10. I exchanged my old car for a new car. After five years without a single holiday, I was privileged to enjoy four holidays in a single year.

My life also transitioned from belittling, critical, judgmental people to uplifting, encouraging, life-giving individuals. I went from sleeping in separate rooms for three whole years to enjoying a close connection with my husband. From walking away feeling hurt by family members, I walked into feeling abundantly connected.

Every bit of those in-between parts was uncomfortable in terms of learning to hold onto my mojo. Holding onto your power is the key to transformation. Holding onto your power is the answer to all your problems. Holding onto your power is the key to your joy.

EXERCISE

Spend a day observing how you feel during the day as you go about your tasks, job, and interactions with others. Be aware of how you are feeling. Do you feel mojo vibes or mojo-less vibes?

You can either journal your observations at the end of the day or make notes as you go through your day. This exercise is fantastic to identify what and who is good for your mojo and where you are giving your mojo away.

1) Check in with yourself at the start of the day. How are you feeling? Are you feeling the mojo vibes, or do you feel the mojo-less vibes?

2) Identify what you are doing or who you are interacting with. Observe how you are feeling. Are you feeling the mojo vibes or mojo-less vibes?

3) If you feel mojo vibes, then fantastic. Make a note of what you were doing or who you were interacting with. If you feel mojo-less vibes, acknowledge your feelings, and shift them with the statement, 'I am holding onto my mojo. All is well and I am protected.' You can change the words to make it more personal. There is no right or wrong way to do this. The most important thing is that you say something to yourself which enables you to hold onto your power.

Process #6

Celebrate You!

Woohoo! You did it. You have discovered the essence of your mojo and have claimed it back. You learnt the power of forgiveness and meditation, and you have learnt how to hold onto your mojo. You have opened your consciousness to self-awareness. How does it feel to know you are this powerful and have all the control you need to transform your life?

How are you going to celebrate the internal work that you had the courage to do? It's one thing for others to acknowledge you, but it's oh so empowering to acknowledge yourself and your successes, whether they are small or large. Acknowledging the small wins and successes soon turns into bigger wins and successes. The more you give yourself the self-praise you deserve, the healthier your sense of yourself becomes.

Every time I passed an exam or achieved something when I was growing up, my dad would take the family out for a meal in a lovely restaurant. No wonder I have always found it easy to learn a new skill or have new experiences, since my brain expects to celebrate. I used to celebrate with food and drink as that is what I grew up doing.

When I changed my relationship to food and drink, I changed the way I celebrated. Now, celebration consists of self-pampering with a facial, a massage, or getting my nails done. I might even go on a little shopping spree, treating myself to a nice outfit, shoes, a bag, perfume, or jewellery. I also like to celebrate with supportive family and friends.

When I sign up a new client, I celebrate my success. When I have achieved a personal goal whether it's in my business, my health, my marriage, something to do with parenting, or in a friendship, I celebrate. When I've held onto my mojo in a challenging situation, I celebrate. When I have maintained a calm, loving, and respectful response to my daughter for an entire week, I celebrate. The same goes for how I treat my husband.

Anchoring your successes, whether with a hand on your heart and a heart-filled thank you, or a punch in the air with a 'yes, I did it' is all part of celebrating yourself. The more times you do this, the more your vibe shifts to a successful vibe, which in turn leads to more success. Be sure to acknowledge yourself and to celebrate because you and your mojo are worth it. Affirm out loud, "I am celebrating my life because I am worth it."

Chapter Two

M is for Mindset

Principle #2

Your Life Experiences Are Created Through Your Mind with Your Thoughts, Feelings, Attitudes, and Beliefs

Every moment offers a unique experience. At this moment you are reading this book, expanding your knowledge. I am typing up this manuscript in my gym restaurant while I sip an almond milk latte. Each moment is unique because it will never come again.

Before I started typing, I enjoyed a swim and a sauna. Before that, I took my daughter to school. An experience isn't just the first time you do something. Every single time you do something, it's an experience, even if you have done something a hundred times over.

We want good health because we want to experience a healthy body. We want wealth because we want to experience enjoying it, giving it, and creating from it. We want to feel joy because we wish to experience our inherent state. We want to enjoy these things because it's friggin great! All of this can happen once we have our mojo back.

Life is an unrepeatable journey of one experience after another. By looking at every moment as an experience, it changes our perception of our lives. In this present moment in my life journey, I am experiencing being a wife to my husband Nick, a mum to my seven-year-wise daughter, a daughter to my parents, and a sister to my younger sister. I am pregnant with my second child. I am also experiencing being an aunty to my niece and nephew, a sister-in-law to my sister's husband, a daughter-in-law to my husband's parents, a customer, a friend, a client to my life coach, a life coach and teacher to my clients and students, an author to my readers. I think you get the picture.

In this present moment, perhaps you are experiencing being a mum as well as other roles in the lives of many people. You are having an experience with your health, wealth, and joy. If you own a business, you are experiencing being a business owner. If you are in a romantic relationship, you are experiencing being a partner to your love. You are having an experience with your finances, with your home, and with your choice of clothes.

Whether you are having good experiences or bad experiences depends on your mindset. Your thoughts, feelings, attitudes, and beliefs all play into this. If you are having mostly good experiences that bring out your joy, you only need to tweak your mindset slightly to match the type of experiences you wish to have. If you are having bad experiences most of the time, there is more to tweak. However, just know that you can jump into the driver's seat of your life and deliberately create the type of experiences you really want by simply doing some internal work on your mindset. How cool is that?

When I realised, I had power to change my own mindset so I could have the experiences I wanted in my life, I was on a high vibe for weeks. Ever heard someone say, 'It's all in your mind'? Well, they are right. It is all in each of our minds.

The way most of us have learned to think is so disempowering. You can tell how someone thinks by what they say. Whether you are complaining, judging, criticising, blaming, fearful, worried, stressed, angry—all of these create disempowering life experiences.

The way we think determines much of the way we feel. Thinking worrying thoughts makes us feel worried. The often-heard statement, 'It's a mother's job to worry' is ridiculous. It took only one human being to say such a disempowering statement, and it then became a part of our mass consciousness. This belief creates a lifetime of worry, coupled with an abundance of worrying situations for our children. Why worry about something that has not happened? If it then happens, you tell yourself, 'See, I knew this was going to happen.' It will happen because you thought it, imagined it, and gave it enough energy to create it.

My clients do not pay me to say what they want to hear. They pay me to tell them what they do not want to hear. They pay me to show them their truth so that they can live their best life possible. I choose to believe, 'It's a mother's job to imagine the best possible outcome.' This generates a lifetime of feeling empowered, along with an abundance of best possible outcomes. I imagine my daughter will inherit this empowering belief and apply it in her own life.

Many parents worry so much about their children that all their worries manifest themselves in everyday life—and then they scold their children for what they created from their worrying. It's a no-win situation for a child with parents who worry so much. Ask my parents!

Our feelings create our attitude toward the world. Our attitude drives the actions we take, which then imprints beliefs from which we create our life experiences. Someone with a disempowering attitude about themselves, such as 'nothing good ever happens to me,' will unconsciously take action that creates the evidence of nothing good ever happening to them. They then observe the evidence and say, 'See, I told you nothing good ever happens to me.' Can you imagine what such a belief does to a person's self-esteem?

Disempowering self-beliefs lead to procrastination, laziness, not bothering, fear of change, fear of trying something new, fear of learning a new skill, doubt about one's abilities—in other words, a powerless sense of self-esteem. A powerless self-esteem fogs up one's mojo. We lose sight of who we truly are.

Someone with an empowering attitude about themselves such as 'life is so good to me' will unconsciously take action that creates evidence of good happening to them. They observe the evidence and say, 'See, life is good to me.' The more they affirm it, the more they take action that creates this result. This eventually becomes an empowering self-belief that builds on their inherently healthy self-esteem.

I want to say a little more about self-esteem. There are two distinct ways of looking at this term. The first is that of the ego. With the ego, we look at ourselves and make a judgment. The key here is that we are looking *at* ourselves, as if we were a character in our own movie. This is how we can praise ourselves one minute and criticise ourselves the next. 'I'm a good person—I'm a bad person.' Which is it? With the ego's view of ourselves, we can never really be sure. Who we are fluctuates with the tides of public opinion.

This is not at all what I mean when I use the term self-esteem. The way I use this term, it has nothing in common with looking *at* ourselves and making a judgment about whether our actions are good or not so good. Self-esteem is a *genuine sense of our goodness* that rises from our essence. It's *feeling* the person we are at our centre, which is always positive.

In the usual way of thinking about self-esteem, we judge ourselves based on *how we perform,* or on how we think we have performed. This is why our evaluation of ourselves can fluctuate from 'fantastic' to 'hopeless' in an instant, often depending on how we think others see us. With true self-esteem, there also a choice to be made. In any given situation, are we going to trust our deeper being, or will we sell ourselves out to what our external world might be saying right now, or what we think people are saying?

When you have authentic self-esteem that rises from your centre, what others say or feel about you matters not a whit. If they point out something you did that can be improved, you do not see this as a reflection on who you essentially are. It has nothing to do with the goodness of your inner being, and you can accept it as an *affirmation* of your goodness. Any momentary lapse is then regarded as an occasion when you failed to heed your essential self. The result is you learn to tune into yourself more deeply.

You can see how your self-esteem affects the vibes you put out. If you're sensitive to vibes like I am, you'll be able to tell whether someone is thinking disempowering thoughts or empowering thoughts. They will either have a positive vibe about them or a negative vibe. I love being around people with positive vibes because I know they are *automatically* thinking empowering thoughts, since these are the only thoughts, they give any attention to. The rest are allowed to fall by the wayside. I find the company of such people to be enjoyable, inspiring, uplifting. I walk away feeling full of energy because being in their presence reminds me of my own positive centre.

When I'm around people who have a negative vibe, I can sense they are thinking disempowering thoughts. I don't enjoy their company and walk away feeling drained. This then affects my vibe and mindset. I catch myself feeling disempowered. I call this vibe contamination. When I realise my vibe has been contaminated, I get straight to work decontaminating it. This enables my authentic self to shine brightly again.

Spending time with people with good vibes is important to me because I want to create fantastic life experiences for myself and my family. Who you spend your time with is important to your life and your mojo.

After observing how I felt around people, I discovered I could handle around two hours with them if they had a negative vibe. As I want to maintain powerful thoughts, powerful feelings, powerful attitudes, and powerful beliefs in order to live a powerful life experience, I learnt to love myself enough to remove myself politely from disempowering people.

I had to make tough decisions with family members who think disempowering thoughts, but I made the decision, and I am a happier woman. My family are happier too, especially my daughter who needs the best version of me so that she can be the best version of herself.

It isn't only the people in our lives who make an empowering or a disempowering impact on our mindset, it's also the TV soaps we watch, the newspapers, social media, the books we read, the internet, and the vibe of the music we listen to. These have a huge effect on our thoughts, feelings, attitudes, and beliefs.

I noticed a big difference in my own mindset when I gave myself a break from social media for nine months, stopped watching soaps, and stopped listening to the news. When I quit reading and listening to anything disempowering, it felt a little uncomfortable for a while. For instance, on a Monday evening my favourite soap was on. The soap featured storylines about people having affairs, drama, conflict, and lots of disempowering situations. It was my favourite soap because subconsciously I resonated with it. We only watch the types of soaps and films that we resonate with. Which soaps, TV shows and films do you watch, and how do you feel during and after watching them? Do you feel empowered or disempowered? Perhaps you feel emotionless.

Attending parties and visiting friends and family was a little uncomfortable at first as I transformed my relationship with food. I was surrounded by people relishing cakes and chocolates. The discomfort was minimal because I had monitored my mindset beforehand.

When I had not yet learnt to manage my mindset, I ate the sugary food even when I did not want to. I would cave in to fit in with the crowd, attempting to be polite because my old belief encouraged me to accept what was offered to me. To turn it down was considered rude. I have no idea where that belief came from, and it does not matter. What is important is that the belief was transmuted into loving myself by choosing healthy life-giving foods and beverage wherever I am. This is the kind of choice that keeps us true to our wonderful self-esteem, our authentic essence.

During uncomfortable times, I consciously chose supportive empowering thoughts such as, 'I love you too much to give you unhealthy food.' The 'you' was of course my essence, the source of my self-esteem. Such statements helped get me through uncomfortable moments, which were just that—moments. They passed quickly and I was left feeling empowered, good about myself, and another step closer to my health and body goals.

Each time I made a conscious attempt to choose thoughts that would help get me through the uncomfortable moments, I felt proud of myself. This self-proud feeling was building my healthy self-esteem and confidence. Those empowering feelings created empowering attitudes such as 'I can do this. This is so simple. It's easy to be healthy and have the body I want!'

This attitude inspired me to take action that supported my deepest desires. I chose fruit, which contained natural sugar, healthy vitamins, and minerals, instead of food containing refined sugar and unhealthy fat. My conscious choice to choose healthy food soon became a subconscious choice. I listened to healthy self-beliefs, which soon became my new lifestyle.

Therefore, I cannot emphasis enough the importance of having the right mindset before changing anything. It's a matter of coming from our authentic self. I saw the importance of choosing my mindset before any diet, my mindset before starting a new exercise regime, my mindset before getting into a relationship, my mindset before learning a new skill, my mindset before making a baby.

Everything we hear, see, touch, taste, or smell goes straight to our subconscious mind and is stored like records in a data system. Even a sneeze or a cough is recorded. The subconscious mind does not have a filter, nor does it have a sense of humour.

Children take the grownups in their life seriously, whether the grownup is joking with them or not. It all goes into the child's data system, and from there into their experiences. This is another reason I take seriously who I surround myself and my daughter with. If even a family member feeds my daughter's subconscious mind with disempowering thoughts, feelings, attitudes, and beliefs, I spend less time with them. The grownups in our children's lives have a bigger impact on their experiences than most of us realise.

To the degree that our experiences are created through our mind with our thoughts, feelings, attitudes, and beliefs, our life reflects our subconscious mind. The good news is that we can undo all the disempowering, limiting thoughts, feelings, attitudes, and beliefs that are stored in the subconscious. It simply takes a conscious attempt to do so. The processes you are practicing from this book are shifting and shaking you at a subconscious level.

My disempowering relationship with my husband, with my friends and family, with food and my body, and with money was all created from my past disempowered mindset. My present reality is empowering. I now have an empowering relationship with my husband, with my friends and family, with food and my body, with money and everything else in my life *because I changed my mindset.*

EXERCISE

You get to control your experiences, and I am so excited to share with you just how to do that. We cannot change others, but we can change how and who we spend our valuable precious time and energy with. Make a list of people you feel good around, and a list of those who cause you to feel disempowered, also including the social media, TV programs, newspapers, and music that is disempowering.

Affirm, 'I imagine the best possible outcome for myself and others. I create an empowering life with an empowered mindset.'

Process #7

Focus on What You DO Want

What are you focussed on? Is it on what you don't want or on what you do want? Focusing on what we don't want is focusing on a problem. Focusing on what we do want is focusing on a solution.

Focusing on what you don't want makes disempowering issues bigger. Don't give your mojo away by putting too much attention on the issues. Some may call it 'brushing it under the carpet.' it is only brushing it under the carpet if you don't focus on the *solution*.

When we focus on what we want, it feels empowering and does wonders for our mojo. Focusing on what we want sets the wheels of creation in motion. Life doesn't know what we want unless we focus on it. Focussing our attention on what we want starts the process of creating a life we will love.

The universe is an all-inclusive universe. If you say, 'I don't want to be tired all the time,' then your focus is on being tired. The results is that you will experience more situations that make you tired. Life loves you and wants to give you everything you are thinking about, feeling about, believing about, and focusing on. If your focus is on being tired all the time, or the fact you are broke or treated badly by people, then that is what you will receive.

It is so important to focus on what you do want. If you focus on being full of energy, having enough money, being surrounded by people who are nice to you, this is what you will receive. It's crucial that your focus is fuelled by empowering thoughts, empowering feelings, an empowering attitude, and empowering beliefs.

If there is an ounce of doubt, worry, or fear, disempowering energy will fuel your focus. Being aware of any disempowering thoughts, feelings, attitudes, and beliefs is crucial. You then have a chance to release anything disempowering and clean up your energy.

The processes in this chapter will help clean up your focus. You will learn how to manage your mind, so that it is set to receive what you want to experience. I am so excited for you because I do these processes all the time. I have experienced and continue to experience more of what I do want and less of what I do not want. The more you do these processes, the experiences you desire will increase.

This is not an overnight fix. All your problems do not magically disappear in an instant, even as they didn't appear in an instant. As they gradually appeared into your life, they will gradually dissipate. The problems will be replaced with experiences that you want and that compliment your mojo.

A few years ago, I wanted to put my daughter into an independent school instead of a state school, not that there is anything wrong with state schools. This was simply my heart's desire. I wanted to be a size 10 instead of a size 18. I wanted a brand-new car instead of my fifteen-year-old car.

I focused on what I wanted with empowering thoughts such as, 'I am looking forward to doing the school run in my size ten body, with my new car, and with a happy child.' I had an empowering attitude of, 'I can do this. Anything is possible. We deserve this.' My belief was, 'Ashani will go to the independent school and we will all be very happy.'

At the time when this was a new desire that had just been birthed, we did not have the money to pay for the school or the car. I was forty pounds away from being a size ten. Every time my focus shifted to my current circumstances, I quickly shifted it back to what I wanted. It took practice to shift my focus and mindset, just like it took practice to learn how to walk, ride a bike, bake a cake, or cook a curry. Whenever disempowering thoughts, feelings, attitudes, and beliefs came into my awareness, I got to the bottom of what my worries, doubts, and fears were. Then I shifted my perception to an empowering mindset that supported my desires.

Many are afraid of being disappointed if they don't get what they want. Have you ever been told not to get excited about something in case it does not happen? The difference between setting yourself up for disappointment and setting yourself up for success is your mindset. If your mind is set to succeed, you will succeed. If your mind is set for disappointment, you will be disappointed. It really is as simple as that.

But simple does not mean it is automatic. Was it easy to learn how to ride a bike? Was it easy to give birth to a baby? Nevertheless, you did it anyway because you wanted your baby and you wanted to learn how to ride a bike.

I wanted the independent school, the new car, and the new body. I managed my mindset. When the thought popped into my conscious awareness, 'What if it doesn't happen?' I simply responded to the thought with, 'If it doesn't happen, it means something better will happen.' This attitude helped me to get as excited, enthusiastic, and into a state of positive expectation. I eventually stopped feeling afraid of disappointment.

Focusing on what you do want with an empowered mindset is a skill that needs to be developed over time. I always tell my clients to start with something small so that their ability to believe grows. When I first started to develop this skill, I started small.

I started with a car parking space close to the entrance of the shopping centre when my daughter was just one year wise. I started to get a car parking space by the entrance. Then I tried to experience a free coffee. A few weeks later when I had in fact forgotten about the free coffee experiment, the shop assistant served me a coffee on the house. Then I moved onto a bunch of pink and yellow flowers, and a few days later my husband came home with a bunch of pink and yellow roses. I never mentioned I wanted flowers—he just appeared with them. Then I moved onto money and focussed on receiving £200. A few weeks later people who owed me money for years got in touch to repay what they owed. As I could see that this was working, my self-belief grew stronger and I started to experience bigger things such as my dream job, the car I wanted, the school we wanted for our daughter, holidays, my body size—and the list goes on.

EXERCISE

This exercise is designed to shift your focus from what you do not want to what you do want. Remember, the universe is an all-inclusive universe, so if you say you want to be less tired, you are asking for tired because the focus is still on tired. If you say, 'I want more energy' then your focus is on energy and that will be your experience.

1) With an empowered mindset, spend the day focusing on what you do want by first noticing what you don't want.

2) When you catch yourself focusing on what you don't want, simply say to yourself, 'That's what I don't want. What do I want instead?'

3) If you're not feeling empowered or excited about what you do want and are still feeling the lack of it, then stop straight away and adjust your mindset to feel empowered about it. Or choose something else to focus on that feels empowering.

For faster results, write down what you want to experience and write down the empowering thoughts, feelings, attitudes, and beliefs that support the experience.

As an example, say to yourself, 'I want to experience…' Perhaps it is a family holiday in Goa for ten nights during the Christmas holidays.

Think thoughts that support the experience. 'I am looking forward to being in a hot country with my family. I see us having a fun time together. I see us on a plane enjoying the travel together. I see us smiling, laughing, playing together, relaxing, having so much fun. I see Ashani making friends and happily playing with other kids at the resort. I see us socialising with lovely people.'

Encourage feelings that support the experience. 'It feels so good to think about our holiday in Goa. I am so excited about our holiday. It feels empowering knowing that we are going to Goa together. We are going to feel relaxed and joyful on our holiday. I love our family holidays so much. I'm so excited about this experience.'

Associate your mindset with attitudes that support the experience. 'We can make this happen. We will be in Goa together for ten nights. We will experience a family holiday in Goa when it's the perfect time for all of us.'

Foster beliefs that support the experience. 'I believe we will be in Goa, India together. I believe we will experience this together, or something better.'

Process #8

Choose Your Thoughts

Do you ever feel like your thoughts are driving you crazy? Do you ever feel as if your head is going to explode with the hundreds of thoughts whizzing around your mind? You are not alone.

The good news is that each of us has total control of our thoughts. No one can get inside our mind and choose our thoughts for us. We can consciously choose the thoughts that we want to dwell on.

Before I learnt that I can consciously choose the thoughts I wanted to think about, I pictured myself going mad from the thoughts that popped into my mind. Humans have what is often referred to as a 'monkey mind.' In chapter one, I mentioned how we think on average 60,000 thoughts a day and are only conscious of 2,000 of them. The rest of the thoughts, 58,000 thoughts a day, are unconscious. It is these that create our experiences.

Every thought has a frequency vibe, which is unique to it. Thoughts with a low vibe are going to create low feelings, which attract similar experiences. Thoughts with a high vibe create high experiences. When someone thinks a lot of disempowering thoughts, they have a disempowering vibe about them. When they think lots of empowering thoughts, they have an empowering vibe about them.

When you first start to observe your thoughts, you may be shocked at how damaging they are to your mojo, and consequently your experiences. Worry not. With consistency and practice consciously choosing to think empowering thoughts, the disempowering thoughts become less and less. Disempowering experiences also decrease as your essence exerts its presence in accordance with your choices.

Each thought sends out an energy. Like a magnet, that energy magnetises it's opposite and equal. Thinking disempowering thoughts frequently magnetises disempowering experiences, whereas thinking empowering thoughts magnetises empowering experiences. The concept is simple, but it requires daily practice until it becomes automatic. Let me assure you, it *will* become automatic, because this is *your essential way of being,* beneath all the fog that has occluded it.

Each thought will draw to it another thought like it. That is how we create momentum with our thoughts. One minute I could be thinking one single thought about going away on a warm holiday, and within a few minutes I have planned out where I'm going, who with, when, the duration of the holiday, where we are going to stay, and even what clothes to pack. This happens because one thought attracts another like it. The more momentum we create, the stronger the energy becomes.

Many create momentum from disempowering thoughts. The result is disempowering experiences. They then say, 'That's just life.' Or they may conclude it's simply 'bad luck.' They then blame the government, the educational system—anyone but themselves. They do this because they do not know how powerful their thoughts are. Neither do they realise that they can turn disempowering experiences around and create a successful, joyful life for themselves by simply choosing empowering thoughts.

What we are focusing our attention on has much influence on the thoughts we are thinking. Most of us have learnt to focus on what we do not want, which starts the momentum of disempowering thoughts, and the result is a mojo-less vibe. This is why I purposely put 'process #7 Focus on what you do want' before this one so that you get into the habit of focusing on what you do want to influence empowered thoughts.

The more we practice focusing on what we do want, the quicker we train the brain to search for what we do want and begin to think empowering thoughts automatically – the result is a mojo vibe.

Deliberately shifting the focus to what we do want makes thinking empowering thoughts a lot easier.

EXERCISE

1) Take a day to have fun with your thoughts.

2) Every time you catch yourself thinking a disempowering thought, say to yourself, 'Thank you for sharing. For now, I choose to think about something fun.' Then choose something empowering to think about—and *milk* it, which means creating momentum around the empowering thing you are thinking about.

3) If your mind wants to wrestle with disempowering thoughts or is being stubborn like mine was when I first started doing this process, you can say, 'I'll think about you later, but for now I'm choosing to think about something fun.' Because I was not completely shutting it down, this calmed my monkey mind.

Remember to observe what you are focusing your attention on while you monitor your thoughts. Be easy with yourself. Try to practice this exercise without self-judgment.

Process #9

You Get What You Feel

I believe life is about giving and receiving. What we give, we receive. If we hurt another, the hurt will return to us. If we love another, we will receive love back. If we blame another, we will be blamed. If we are kind to another, we will receive kindness.

How you feel this moment is in large measure a manifestation of the thoughts you have been thinking about. However, it used to be thought that all emotion is caused by what we think—and now we know this simply is not true. Pure emotion can arise spontaneously, and our thoughts kick in to exacerbate what we feel. Studies have shown that if we allow emotions to move through our body without resisting them, it normally takes as little as ninety seconds for an emotion to pass. The reason emotions can take days or weeks—or at times months or years—to pass is that we *feed* them with our thoughts about them.

The point of developing our ability to feel is that we want to *feel the whole of life*, not truncating any of our feelings. If we do not permit ourselves to feel what's occurring within us, its effects tend to get stuck in our body, which eventually manifests in depression, physical pain, or undesirable experiences.

We call our emotions 'feelings,' when in reality there may be a huge difference between an emotion we are experiencing and what we are feeling deep within us. Emotions can block the deeper feelings of the heart. You can be so 'in love' with someone, but moments later when they do something you don't like, you can find yourself yelling, 'I hate you and never want to see you again.' The emotion of the moment is different from the deeper feelings of the heart.

To get a clear picture of the difference between emotions and feelings, consider a couple who hire a babysitter for Valentine's Day and go out for a romantic dinner. On the drive back from the restaurant, they get into a disagreement over whether their daughter is to go to into the law or study to be a doctor when she graduates from high school. The argument escalates to where the two end up on opposite sides of the bed with a wide no-man's land between them. What are they *feeling*?

The emotion unleashed in such an argument screams, 'Get away from me. Stay on your own side of the bed—in fact, go sleep on the couch! Do not dare touch me. Don't even say a word.'

But what is the feeling beneath the emotion? The feeling, which is being eclipsed by the force of the emotional reaction, is that both wish this argument had never happened and that they could resolve it and reconnect.

Says the heart, 'I wish you'd reach out. I wish I could reach out. I hate feeling upset with you like this.' But the emotion counters angrily, 'You better not reach out—or I'll push your hand away. And I'm not going to reach out because you might push my hand away.' There will be no intimacy that night, nor for the next several nights.

Emotions can come together with such force that they totally eclipse head and heart, in the process producing a pseudo clarity. Sadly, while we were growing up, few of us were taught the difference between insight and thoughts, feelings, and emotional reactions.

Emotions can be produced by deep feeling. They can also mask our feelings, as we have just seen. Our deeper feelings always guide us and let us know whether we are on the right path.

Feelings and emotions are magnetic because an emotion is simply energy moving through the body. Motion means movement, and the 'e' in emotion is for energy. All an emotion consists of is energy moving through the body. I learnt this from the documentary on DVD, E-motion. Our emotions and feelings are a gift because they guide us and create our experiences. If you feel anger, energy is moving through your body. If you feel excited, that too is energy. Energy in motion (emotion) is magnetic. Be sure you only feed those emotions that are in line with your deeper feelings, not those transient emotions that erupt, eclipse our true feelings, and left to themselves in no time die away unless we add thought to them.

When my daughter Ashani expresses a powerless emotion, I know immediately that she has encountered a powerless experience. As I understand after researching for many years about the mind, how we feel subconsciously plays a very big part in the experiences we attract.

With this understanding, I can help her to acknowledge her emotions and provide a safe space for her to feel them so that they can pass through her and not get stuck for a lifetime, becoming the set point for all her future experiences. I can then support her to move from feeling disempowered slowly but surely to feeling empowered again. Patience, love, and understanding are needed because there can be a big gap from feeling sad to feeling love again.

Esther and Jerry Hicks author of *The Astonishing Power of Emotions* created an emotional guidance scale. You will see below right at the top of the list is Joy/Appreciation/Empowered/Freedom/Love.

As you go down the list, you will notice the lower-level emotions Fear/Greif/Depression/Despair/Powerlessness. The jump from disempowered to empowered is way too big.

Emotional Guidance Scale

1) Joy/Appreciation/Empowered/Freedom/Love

2) Passion

3) Enthusiasm/Eagerness/Happiness

4) Positive Expectation/Belief

5) Optimism

6) Hopefulness

7) Contentment

8) Boredom

9) Pessimism

10) Frustration/Irritation/Impatience

11) Overwhelmed

12) Disappointment

13) Doubt

14) Worry

15) Blame

16) Discouragement

17) Anger

18) Revenge

19) Hatred/Rage

20) Jealousy

21) Insecurity/Guilt/Unworthiness

22) Fear/Grief/Depression/Despair/Powerlessness.

To tell a child who is feeling disempowered to get a grip or to snap out of it is asking the impossible. A child will feel even more powerless because they do not know how to 'snap out of a feeling'. You cannot just snap out of a feeling.

You can acknowledge a feeling, release it, and feel a better feeling, but you cannot just snap out of it. And what does 'get a grip' even mean? Get a grip of what? Your emotions? How? Ridiculous. We say these ridiculous statements when we don't know how to emotionally support someone who is in emotional pain.

To ignore a child who is feeling sad and low, or in a sulk, is teaching them to stuff their emotions down and to put a lid on them. It is not teaching them to be emotionally intelligent. In fact, it is teaching them to be emotionally immature.

This is the reason there are so many adults who do not know how to manage their emotions and who are emotionally immature because they were emotionally neglected at a critical learning time in their childhood. They are in emotional pain. This is one of the most common reasons for suicide, depression, low self-esteem, and a lack of positive self-belief.

Supporting a child and ourselves to move up the emotional guidance scale inch by inch is one of the most loving and intelligent things we parents can do. Denying their emotions and our own is a dangerous game to play. Emotions and feelings are nothing to be afraid of.

It is not wrong to feel what we have been created with. They exist to guide us through life, to navigate around the good and the bad. How else would my daughter know she was in a dangerous situation if I had shut down her emotions? How can she ever feel worthy if she is not allowed to feel emotion?

Children are not stupid. They know when they are being loved as a whole person, tears, snot, and all. They know when they are being loved only on the condition that they do not express emotions. This is not love. This is control.

Every emotion is important and needed to navigate through life. We get what we feel especially from our disowned emotions that are stuck in our subconscious.

To witness my daughter thriving in life because she feels worthy and good about herself makes my heart smile, and I feel like a proud mum. Certificates and awards are great but temporary. Emotional intelligence is a life-long reward of satisfying and fulfilling experiences. Nothing tangible can bring more joy than that.

EXERCISE

1) Spend a day observing how you are feeling as you go about your daily activities and when you are interacting with people.

2) Every hour or so stop what you are doing and check in with yourself by asking, 'How am I feeling right now?'

This exercise will bring awareness to the kind of thoughts you are thinking, whether consciously or unconsciously. It also gives you an indication of what is coming your way in the future. Your thoughts and feelings are creating your future experiences. Choose them wisely.

Process #10

What Do You Believe In?

As well as your thoughts and feelings, your beliefs also play an important part in creating your experiences. Our choices and actions in large measure stem from our beliefs. If we believe that raising children is hard, we interpret it as hard and subconsciously make choices that make raising children difficult. If we believe that raising children is enjoyable, we see it as enjoyable and make conscious choices that make it enjoyable.

We each have a bunch of beliefs that are either empowering or disempowering. We also have family beliefs, which are called 'paradigms.' Family beliefs get passed down from generation to generation. Our beliefs encompass relationships, family, raising children, money, career, spirituality, health, wealth, and in fact every area of life. These paradigms either benefit us or are the cause of unwanted experiences.

Take a disempowering belief as an example. If you have been told that once you become a mum, you will lose your mojo, this belief will create a disempowering experience of motherhood. Being a mother will feel like drudgery.

Life is constantly evolving, so our beliefs also need to evolve if we are to live a joyous life. Unfortunately, many of our paradigms are out of date. For instance, our children were born into a world of iPads and smart phones. When we were born, our homes had a TV that was a little box with four channels. Our parents were born into a world where they had rationing. Our grandparents were born when nappies were handwashed. No one had ever heard of a disposable nappy.

If our paradigms come from when there was no such thing as a disposable nappy, and women were not allowed to work and generate an income of their own, off course we would believe that raising children is hard. These old beliefs do not serve us today. Times have changed, and it is time to change our beliefs to create joyful experiences.

What do you believe about yourself? Do you believe you are perfect just as you are? Do you believe you are a powerful being? Do you believe you are always supported by life? Do you believe you are an amazing, wonderful mother? Do you believe you are a beautiful soul who deserves an abundance of good health, wealth, and joy?

Your beliefs generate feelings because a belief is a manifestation of a repeated thought. If you feel feelings of jealousy, insecurity, resentment, revenge, worry, doubt, or fear, you are harbouring a disempowering belief.

What we believe about ourselves is subconsciously projected onto our children and anyone we love. This occurs automatically, unless we become aware of how our beliefs affect those we care about. When our children are in relationships of their own, if we project our insecurities onto them, we can create issues in their romantic lives and have no idea we are doing so.

We also subconsciously project our experiences onto others. When I was pregnant with Ashani, friends and family were projecting their terrible birthing experiences onto me, telling me how painful it is and how it is the worst experience I'll have in my life.

I consciously and in the silence of my mind refused to believe that my experience would be like theirs. I chose to believe that my experience would be a beautiful one. I chose to believe that my experience will be so amazing that even midwives would talk about my labour to others.

With this empowering mindset of positive thoughts, feelings, attitudes, and beliefs about my labour experience, life presented to me the resources that supported my beliefs. When the day came to give birth to my beautiful baby girl, I was totally relaxed and had the most peaceful and calm labour. Ashani came into the world calmly and peacefully.

My sister was giving birth to her baby boy just a few months later and her midwife told her about this woman who meditated through her labour. She was talking about my experience just like I believed would happen.

Just because people have had experiences before we have experienced them, whether it's giving birth for the first time, getting married, buying a house, having a second child, hitting menopause, it doesn't mean we have to believe that their experience will be ours. We can choose what we wish to believe about ourselves and the world, creating our own unique experiences that are personal to us.

Now that I am expecting my second child, friends and family are subconsciously projecting their experiences on to me. It is harder with the second, they say. You don't get any time to yourself, they say. I listen, nod, and smile politely, and in the silence of my mind say, 'I don't choose that experience. I choose a satisfying and fulfilling family life experience.'

A repeated thought becomes a belief. If we tell ourselves something enough times, before we know it, it has become a subconscious belief. So, I say thank you to all my fear-mongering friends and family because each time they project their disempowering beliefs onto me, it gives me the opportunity to repeat my choice of experience, which will eventually become a belief.

When we instil positive self-beliefs, we automatically and naturally instil positive self-beliefs into our children. Tell a child 'you are naughty' enough times and eventually it becomes a self-belief 'I am naughty.' They subconsciously behave like a naughty child until they change that lie. Tell a child, 'You are a great kid' enough times, and it will become their self-belief, so that they subconsciously behave like a great kid.

I hear adults saying, 'I am so stupid!' after repeating this lie to themselves several times, it becomes their subconscious belief and they feel insecure about themselves for the rest of their lives unless they are lucky enough to be taught how to change that lie to the truth of their essence, which is extremely intelligent. They make excuses such as they did not have good teachers at school, or they were born that way. These are further lies to cover up the first lie that they are stupid.

We do not have to be who we don't want to be. We can be anything and anyone we want to be through empowering self-belief, which is our truth.

EXERCISE

This exercise will bring awareness to your subconscious beliefs and family paradigms. You can decide whether your beliefs are out of date or in alignment with the type of life you desire.

For faster results write down your answers to the questions below.

1) Spend a day paying attention to which areas in your life you would love to improve.

2) Ask yourself, 'What are my beliefs about this area?'

3) Ask yourself, 'What beliefs do I need to have to improve this aspect of my life?'

4) Create a new belief and repeat it as a mantra while you meditate first thing in the morning and last thing at night.

Remember a belief is simply a repeated thought. Watch your thoughts especially about yourself.

Process #11

Positive Pictures

One of the most helpful tools we have been born with is our imagination and its ability to create visuals. With our inbuilt paintbrush, we have the power to paint our own internal pictures of how we wish to experience our life. I cannot tell you strongly enough how vital this is in our quest to bring about what we wish to achieve.

The images we create and project out into the universe create our reality. Before you had a family of your own, you most probably had images in your mind of holding your baby in your arms. When we think thoughts, our mind automatically creates a visual of this thought.

You can put it to the test. Think of a pink elephant. Did you see an image of a pink elephant flash in your mind? It is so quick, like a flash. I call these snapshot visuals. We have snapshot visuals all day, every day, because we think thoughts all day.

Our experiences are created from the thoughts we think, the feelings we feel, the beliefs we hold, and the images we create in our mind. These are the main four tools that make up the mind's creative potential. Until we become conscious of our thoughts, feelings, attitudes, and beliefs, our thoughts are thinking us, our feelings are evoking emotions, our beliefs are making us miserable, and the images in our mind consist of worry, doubt, and fear. Until we wake up, we are walking around asleep. We live life by default. Until we wake up, our mojo is fast asleep.

Do you remember being a child and dreaming up pictures in your mind of a magical Christmas? Or maybe you dreamt of running away from home. Whatever you desired, you made up images in your mind. When they happened, it was magical.

Many of us stop imagining and dreaming when we become mothers. Why? We stop dreaming because we believe that after having a family of our own, we were supposed to live happily ever after like Snow White, Cinderella, and every story or film we saw when we were growing up. For some reason we fell for the assumption that when we reached a certain point in our lives, it was all going to be rainbows and lollipops. The outcome was that we lost our identity. As I experienced, it was as if our mojo had simply vanished. We felt lost, as if life had cheated us of any chance of being happy ever after.'

The truth is that being 'happy ever after' is not a pipe dream, it's a reality we experience when we live from our centre.

Creating positive pictures for ourselves, our children, our partners, and all our loved ones begins in our essence, from which we create empowering feelings. Our images fuel feeling, which is the most magnetic and fastest way to create any life experience we wish to enjoy.

When you take a glimpse into your past, what pictures do you see? Are they pictures of pain and misery, or are they pictures of joy and love?

When you think of your future, do you see pictures of an abundance of health, wealth, and joy, or do you see pictures of loneliness and illness?

We project our past onto our future. Our pictures of the future create our present mindset. This is huge, and it is important we grasp this concept.

If we look at our childhood and see pictures of a dysfunctional family, which apparently is true of 85% of families, then we subconsciously expect our family to be dysfunctional in the future. That subconscious image of the future will create the mindset in the present to be set to create a dysfunctional family in the future. This is how powerful our mind is.

With this understanding, I only choose to focus on the good experiences in my past that create the positive pictures in my mind of a fantastic childhood with so many beautiful memories. Because I consciously choose to create positive pictures of the past, I subconsciously see a positive future, and it is this positive future that I subconsciously expect as I create my present mindset.

My daughter loves listening to me talk about my past and I love to share positive stories with her. She asks me often, 'Mummy, tell me a story of when you were little.' I share exciting, adventurous, and fun stories. When I speak of my family or my husband's family, I only share positive stories. When I talk of the future, I share the positive and the dreams I wish to create.

Our children are listening to us and watching us all the time as they learn about the world and program their minds to match the programming of our minds. By sharing positive stories of my past, my daughter is seeing positive pictures and her brain is being programmed to search for positive stories of the past, present, and future. It is fascinating to watch her have positive experiences naturally without even trying.

A powerful exercise you can do with your children at bedtime is to talk about all the good things that happened that day. Your children will search their minds for positive pictures and feel good.

Going to sleep for the night with positive pictures and feeling good will give your children a good night's sleep and they will wake up feeling positive. The same goes for us. What we think about as we fall asleep goes round and round like a stuck record all night long in our sleep.

EXERCISE

Spend a day, dreaming up positive pictures of your past and future and enjoy the mojo vibes as you watch the pictures in your mind all day long.

Before you follow the steps below, close your eyes, put your dominant hand on your heart, and breathe deeply and slowly in and out three times for your subconscious to open and to connect to your essence.

1) Take a glimpse into your past and search your database for positive pictures. Hold the pictures in your mind and enjoy them for as long as your mind can hold onto them. Write down the top three positive experiences.

2) Have a peak into your future and create three positive pictures. Hold the pictures in your mind and enjoy them for as long as your mind can hold it. Write down what the three positive experiences are.

3) Now become present and write down how it felt to see positive pictures from your past and future.

Process #12

Celebrate Your Mindset!

Congratulations! Becoming a master of your own mind is a total game changer and life transforming. Keep practicing the processes you have learnt from this chapter daily. What you have learnt about your mindset, your thoughts, feelings, attitudes, and beliefs has expanded your consciousness and awareness. You will soon witness positive changes in your life.

Your mindset will soon be set to create a satisfying and fulfilling family life. You are that powerful. You are that smart!

To anchor your success, expanding your consciousness and your awareness of your true self is a huge achievement.

Celebrate your powerful mindset. Celebrate you. Celebrate the positive role model you are for your children.

Treat yourself, pamper yourself, and do what feels good to you because you and your mind are worth it.

You can even celebrate every day as you practice a process a day. I am celebrating with a punch in the air and a long soak in the tub tonight for writing up chapter two and for having the courage to share my vulnerable personal stories with you.

Affirm out loud, 'I am celebrating my success because I deserve it.'

Chapter Three

A is for Action

Principle #3

The Most Joyful Journey Through Life Is Created by Taking Inspired Action

This principle makes being a mum so much fun. In fact, it makes being human fun. Imagine a life without struggle, suffering, and sorrow. I am not saying that you will never face challenges, obstacles, the washing machine breaking down, or a leak in the roof. These kinds of problems only turn into a struggle, suffering, and sorrow if we allow our minds to dwell on them. They are part of life, and life just happens.

Imagine if such moments were few and far between, with almost every day filled with fun and excitement. Wouldn't that be amazing?

Imagine if the journey to fabulous health, abundance of wealth, lots of happiness, and getting your mojo back came naturally to you. Imagine if getting out of debt, shedding weight, having a close connection with your spouse, and raising your children was exhilarating. From my own experience of personal growth and development, understanding how life naturally responds to our mindset when we take daily action steps, life *is* friggin joyous. Can you believe, the journey to my weight loss was nothing but joyous from beginning to end?

The journey to finding a close loving connection with my husband was pure joy. The journey to creating the family holidays, manifesting a car, a fun social life, family and friends, and my dream career have been nothing but joyous. Okay, I cried a few tears at times and felt some icky emotions, but I did not take out a mortgage in self-pity. I used the techniques that I am going to give you in the next chapter to move out of those icky emotions and jump back into joy.

Life experiences and life lessons are all a significant contribution to our growth and are part of our journey. The path we walk on may be bumpy, smooth, hard, easy, stressful, peaceful, and everything in between.

For some their path consists of stress, stress, stress. For some their path is depressing, dull, and boring. For some their path is dangerous and full of drama. For some their path is adventurous, exciting, and fun. For some their path is pristine, narrow, and serious. For some their path is peaceful and joyous.

I have not met anyone yet who wants a stressful, depressing, or dull path. I certainly do not, and I am pretty sure you don't either. Stress, dullness, and depression harm your self-esteem and confidence. They do absolutely nothing for your mojo.

A stressful path creates more experiences to stress about. It is a vicious cycle that holds you back from learning lessons, and I believe it stunts emotional and personal growth.

Choosing a path of joy creates more experiences that bring increased joy. When we choose joy every time instead of stress and anything else that is disempowering, we become willing to learn the lessons that add value to us as a person and build emotional intelligence and personal growth. Each decision for joy is in line with our essential being.

Many of us seek joy in the cream cake, a bottle of wine, cigarettes, drugs, gambling, overspending, a heavy night out. This joy is temporary because usually the next day we wake up with a hangover, a sore throat, feeling unattractive, with zero left in our bank account, and find we have gained weight. The brain automatically searches for another quick fix. This path is a stressful, frustrating, disempowered path filled with little pockets of joy that are few and far between.

The most joyful journey through life is created by taking inspired action. When we take action that is fuelled by inspiration, the action feels fun, time goes fast while we take the action, and the results are joyful.

When we force ourselves to take some kind of action toward our goals and desires by using willpower, life is harder. The goal feels like it's a huge mountain to climb. Before we know it, we come tumbling down, only to start all over again. After ten, twenty, or thirty or more proven years of starting again, we eventually give up on the goal and make up lies like, "I just love food and my whole family love food, so I'm never going to be slim." Or we may conclude, "It's too late for me. It's all about my children now."

The truth is these people have given up on their dream of being healthy, wealthy, and living a life of joy. They settle for a path filled with rare pockets of happiness, just like I used to until I learnt how to tune into my essence.

I call taking action as a result of willpower, force, or motivation *'ego* action'. When it comes from the ego, there will be an agenda behind the goal such as wanting to achieve the goal to prove to others how good we are. This stems from a feeling of not being good enough. Or we take ego action to get something from the outside such as attention, praise, and recognition so we can feel worthy or smart. This stems from a feeling of unworthiness. The problem with this is that no matter how much we achieve in life, if the desires and action are coming from the ego and a subconscious feeling of unworthiness, not being good enough, or not being loved, the outcome of the achievement will not be enough. After a few hours or a few days of feeling great from other people's recognition and praise, we go back to that empty feeling.

When the desires come from the heart and an inner 'knowing,' and we are connected to our mojo at the same time, the inspiration we experience pulls us strongly to take action toward our heartfelt desires with absolutely no strings, no attachments, no lack, and no agenda.

We take the inspired action because we just cannot ignore the exciting and knowing feeling it brings us. We do well and have fun along the journey to the desire without any need for attention, praise, or recognition from other people.

When it's an inspired idea from our essence, from our connection to our mojo, it's for us and only us. We do it for our personal pleasure and not to fill any void, because we are already feeling satisfaction and fulfilment within ourselves.

When we receive the attention, recognition, and praise for our inspired creations, we feel humbled and appreciative as we know that the credit for our creations also goes to our essence, the source of the inspiration. This is co-creating and it's magical.

My clients ask me how will they know if it's an inspired action or an ego action that they are pulled to? The answer is that the inspired action will feel so right and so exciting that even if you can't find the logic for taking the action, nothing will stop you from taking it.

If it is from the ego, there will be a lot of thinking about it. We will ask, 'What if this, what if that, what will I get, how much will I make?' It will become about money, pleasing others, and doing it for an external reason. It may also take a long time to take action. Then we will tell ourselves, 'Oh, this is hard work. This is stressful.'

When I stopped listening to others and quit trying to please everyone else, I started to listen to my intuition, my essence, and said 'yes' to every inspired desire and action. There were people in my life who were not supportive of my decisions, especially my inspired choice of career. I did not care anymore. I was done with feeling stress and giving up most of my day to sit behind a desk. It simply did not make me happy. It made me money, but it did not make me happy. Sometimes we have to be okay with upsetting others and being the reason for their judgments and gossip. I had to be okay with it. The inspired ideas felt too good to sacrifice for everyone else's happiness.

I was inspired to marry my man. I was inspired to have a child. I was inspired to become a life coach. I was inspired to write this book. As I took the exciting action steps, which came from inspiration, it was all so effortless and oh so fun.

I followed the processes that I share in this book with you every single day until they became a part of my DNA, and today they are my default. You will find that the more you practice the processes, the more in tune with your mojo you will become, and the inspiration will keep on coming. All you have to do is say *'yes'*.

In the course of the next few pages, I give you a bunch of fun processes to connect to that will inspire you. You can start practicing these straight away. But first I need your commitment that you are fully committed to a path of joy. For the processes to work, life requires you to commit to a joyous journey through life.

Process #13

Make a Decision

'Should I, or shouldn't I? I will start tomorrow. No, actually I'll start next week.' How many times do we do this to ourselves when we really want something, and we can't decide if it's the best thing to do?

How many times have you tried to start that diet or gym routine, and it took months just to pack the gym bag? I am guilty of this. How many times have you had the thought, 'I'm going to start that project tomorrow.' A year later, you are still having the same thought. I am guilty of this too.

Fear, doubt, and worry usually are the mind-gremlins that like to jump out and present us with all the reasons we should not do something. Have you noticed those little gremlins? My gremlins were not so little. They were huge monsters that stopped me from having my ideal body and even kept me from writing this book.

Every time I wanted to make a decision that would result in having my ideal body, wealth, and a joyful life, those gremlins gave me all the reasons not to go for my dreams. I had to get past the mind-gremlins by reassuring them that I was safe, and they would usually quiet down for a few minutes. But it wasn't long before they started screaming at me to stop. A little reassurance again, until they trusted that I had my highest good in mind and that of everyone else, and they eventually stepped aside and let me take the driver's seat.

Being safe is at the top of the priority list for our brain, so go easy with your mind-gremlins as they are only trying to protect you. Once they are reassured, you are ready to go.

What happens after making a decision is pretty amazing. Your path starts to unfold right before your eyes, bit by bit as soon as you make a decision. But the decision must come straight from your heart. A heartfelt, meaningful decision with conviction is necessary if it is to have any energy behind it. Life will totally support your decision and will present you with everything you need to fulfil your desires.

Once I made a decision with conviction to be a size ten, by the end of the year my body knew that I friggin meant it. With all my heart I said, 'I have decided, I am going to be a size ten by the end of this year. I am not stopping until I have reached my goal, and nothing is going to derail me.'

Before that day, I made a half-hearted decision which was filled with fears, doubts, and worries. This resulted in failing every attempt at releasing the weight. In fact, I would end up gaining weight.

This happened with my career too. Every time I made a decision with my mind-gremlins screaming at me, I ended up failing. When we make a decision with our mind-gremlins whispering their fears, doubts, and worries in the back of our mind, we can't hear our intuition, which emerges from our essence giving us the steps we need to take.

If we can make a decision to eat that blueberry muffin and relish every bite, we can also make a decision to write that book until it's published. We can make the decision to declutter the house until the entire house is rid of all the clutter. We can make the decision to brush our teeth with our little ones every evening until they have formed the habit of brushing teeth twice a day.

From my own experience, the best time to make a decision is after quieting our mind-gremlins. At such moments, we feel good about the decision. We affirm the decision audibly. Life will hear us, and before we know it, it will present our first step.

Life will not show you the entire path, otherwise those mind-gremlins will freak out. Your only job is to say 'yes' to the first step, then get to work. But first you must make the decision.

EXERCISE

Spend a day thinking about what you need to feel satisfied and fulfilled. Is it a healthy body? Is it more wealth? Is it more joy in your relationships? Get clear with what you need and make a decision to make it happen.

1) Close your eyes, take three breathes in and out deeply and slowly.

2) With your eyes closed and your body completely relaxed with a calm energy, ask yourself, 'What do I need in my life to feel satisfied and fulfilled?'

3) Listen to your thoughts. Whatever comes up for you, try not to reject it. Be honest with yourself without self-judgment.

4) Make the decision with conviction and energy to have it.

Write this down for faster results:

I have decided that I am

_____

Process #14

The Meaningful Why

We are not compelled to quiz ourselves when we want or need something. We are much more likely to quiz our children, finding out why they want to borrow money or the reason they want a particular toy.

Why do you want your mojo back? Why do you want to live a satisfying and fulfilling life? When you start questioning your desires, you naturally evoke good feelings. I wanted to release weight because I wanted to feel good in my body. I wanted a wealth of friends because I feel good when I'm socialising. I wanted more money because it feels good to be able to get anything my daughter needs. I wanted a new car because it feels good to know we are safer in a reliable car. I wanted a closer connection with my husband because it feels good to know I'm secure in my relationship.

When we know why we want what we want, we start feeling good before we receive it. That good feeling then inspires an action step. Allow yourself to feel what it would feel like to have your mojo back, to be in good health, to be wealthy, to live in joy. Make a list of all the reasons you want these things.

At first you may think of the obvious. For instance, let's say you want to release weight. Your reason may be because you want to be slim. This is where most people stop. If you continue to question your reasons, you will eventually find much more meaningful reasons come up. Here is what my self-quizzing to release my weight looked like:

Why do I want to be forty pounds lighter? Because I want to be slim

Why do I want to be slim? Because I want to wear clothes that I actually like

Why do I want to wear clothes that I like? Because I want to look good

Why do I want to look good? Because I want to feel good about myself

Why do I want to feel good about myself? Because I want to be more confident

Why do I want to be more confident? Because it will improve my relationships, social life, business. I will feel good at parties and events.

Why else do I want to be forty pounds lighter? Because I will be healthy and fit

Why do I want to be healthy and fit? Because I will be more active and live longer

Why do I want to be more active and live longer? Because I want more energy to play with Ashani, and I want her to have a mum in her life for as long as she can.

And there it was. My deep, meaningful reason for wanting to be slimmer. By questioning every reason, I eventually got down to the deeper drive that created the feeling I needed to release the weight.

Your job is to remind yourself of the why as much as possible. Every morning and every night are the best time to contemplate your reasons for what you want. It is the why that evokes inspiration. Whenever I think about why I want to write this book, I start thinking of all the meaningful reasons. It feels so empowering, exciting, and I end up feeling inspired to write.

The inspiration is so intense that I can't not take action. I remember when I first was inspired to write this book, I would become so inspired by thinking of all the meaningful reasons for writing, I would end up buying a notepad if I was out and going straight to a café to spend hours writing away.

Inspired action never feels like work. It never feels draining. It never feels forced. It feels so good that we just do not want to stop. The best thing about taking action when we are inspired is that the results end up being incredible. Every time I have acted from inspiration, I have looked back at what I have created and end up feeling amazed with myself. I literally cannot believe that I created whatever it was that I created from inspiration.

Find your *why* for whatever you want. Not the obvious why, but the deep and meaningful why. The real reason feels good in every fibre of your being. This is the why that you truly desire, and this is what will create the inspiration you need.

EXERCISE

I invite you to spend a day quizzing yourself as to why you want your mojo back, and why you want to live a satisfying and fulfilling family life.

Keep questioning every reason until you find your meaningful why. You will know it's right because it will be the one that creates a deep feeling in you.

For faster results, write it down. I know you are a busy mum. While you go through this book, if doing this in your mind works for you, that is a first step. There should never be a sense of pressure. I think you are brave to open yourself up to do these processes. Not everyone has the guts to go within and take responsibility for their own joy, so please acknowledge yourself. You are one of the few who will put in this work and who will see amazing results.

Process #15

Making Friends with Your Future You

Imagine your life six months from now. What would you love your life to look like? How are you dressed? How is your demeanour? Who are you with? How do you feel about yourself? Imagine you have your mojo back and you are feeling amazing.

Now imagine your life twelve months from now. What are your surroundings? How do you feel about yourself? What are you doing? How is your self-esteem?

Our brain automatically goes to the past, then the present, and finally to the future. It does this all day, every day. A good way to fog up our mojo is to live in the past and reminisce about all the hurt we have suffered. The problem with that is we can't change what people have done to us. An irrational part of us seems to think that if we keep remembering the hurt, talking about it, we will be able to talk and think our way out of it.

Thinking and talking about past hurt only drains our energy, as well as the energy of the people we are complaining to. Resentment of the past only creates experiences that create more resentment in the future. The only thing that can change the past is a change of perception about whatever hurt us.

A new perception gives us a sense of relief from past hurt, which frees us to experience inner peace. Instead of trying to figure why someone did what they did, a process that I use on my past hurt works for me. Give it a go—it might work for you. All I do is I detach the behaviour from the person, so it's no longer about the person and all about the behaviour.

Then I evaluate the behaviour, whether it was words that were said or a physical act. Instead of saying, "She hurt me," it has now become, "Those words that were said to me hurt my feelings." Next, I detach the feelings of hurt from the words. So now I can evaluate just the words that were spoken to me. Now they might look like, "What a daft thing to say to someone."

By this point, the feeling of hurt starts to shift. I can now see that it was nothing personal, just a daft thing to say. People have a choice to speak kind words or words that are not so kind. If someone said unkind things, remember it was their choice to be an unkind person. It is none of our business how others choose to show up in the world.

So at this point after breaking it down, I take the lesson and the gift. The lesson is not to take things personally, especially from people who choose to be daft, either by being insulting, critical, or belittling. I can simply accept them as they are. My gift is that I have just become a better person because I have learnt to be mindful of my communication with others.

Feeling joyful about our future creates an even more joyful future. Worrying about the future creates additional worry. We have more control over our lives than we give ourselves credit for. We cannot create a future for others, but we can imagine a joyful future for them. We cannot control another's mindset, although we can exert a positive influence on them.

Our children are watching and learning from us. Their brains take it all in. How we respond to life and respond to each other greatly influences their behaviour. They see how we deal with life, the choices we make, and how we go about making those choices. They tend to mimic our mindset until they realise, they have control over their own mind and can think for themselves.

When we imagine a future we would love, it provides us with a vision to focus on. The more often we imagine our future, whether it be six months or six years from now, we make friends with it. In my six-week Magnetise your Dream Lifestyle Program, I teach a process to connect with the future you. As we imagine the future, the process of doing this eventually, not always immediately, ignites inspiration within us to take some sort of action to move toward this future.

As we focus on the future self, we start to become this *unconsciously*. This is intense and is my favourite thing to do every single day. My soul and my future self are the two companions I have with me my entire life's journey, from birth to death, so I connect with them both daily. I am never alone—and neither are you, my sweet friend.

If this is the first time you are imagining your future self, go easy with yourself. It takes a few goes to get a clear picture of who you will become. The more you go to the future in your mind, you may add or remove from the vision anything you want. The more you do this, the clearer you become of what you really need to feel happy. When you go to the future, be generous with yourself. Don't hold back because of current circumstances. Open your mind and dream like a child without limitations.

One thing will prevent this process from igniting inspiration, and this is lack of belief. If there is a lack of belief, then the mind-gremlins have woken up. They will tell you this will not work, this is impossible, you cannot have this, get real, this is bullshit, don't be so silly, you'll be disappointed—and anything else that stops you from believing you can be anything you deep down want to be.

Remember to be loving and friendly with the mind-gremlins. Let them gently know that you're just having some fun, and all will be well. Tell them anything that keeps them from sabotaging your future.

You can even communicate with your future you and ask her what your next step should be toward your future. You will either receive the step straight away, or you may receive the inspired action step in a few days. Your only job is to say 'yes,' even if the mind-gremlins are freaking out. If the inspired action feels exhilarating and you have a feeling of knowing it is the right thing to do, say 'yes' and do it.

Eventually, you will realise that you have become your future you, and you might look back and think, 'Wow, I didn't even feel the change.' It is a beautiful thing to make friends with your future you. I believe this process could help so many children to stay focused on a path that brings them joy and empowerment.

EXERCISE

Spend a day trying this process out for yourself. It is one thing reading this book, but physically doing the processes makes the difference.

1) Spend a day, dreaming about a future you would love to experience.

2) See yourself in six to twelve months' time.

3) Use all your senses while you imagine your future you. Think about what you can see, smell, taste, hear, and touch.

4) Make the image so big that you feel like you are standing inside the image.

5) When you feel like your image is starting to fade away, it is time to take a deep breath in and out. Gradually bring your awareness back to your physical body, while you slowly open your eyes.

6) Check in with yourself. How did it feel to imagine your future self this way?

7) Do this as often as you can during the day, and especially tonight while you rest in bed and relax your body, mind, and soul.

Process #16

Imagine it Already Done

This process is one of the most important in terms of inspiration, a joyful journey through life, and to get the results you want. Imagining life as if you have already created what you wanted to create gets you into the "feeling" state you originally sought to experience. When you get into this feeling state, the ideas, the intuitive hits, and the nudges you need start to come through.

Most of us have learnt to go through life by default, so that whatever happens is just the way things are. The truth is if we do not know where we are going, we get lost and waste a lot of precious time. When we are crystal clear about the end result, we are striving for, we can clearly imagine it in the privacy of our own mind. We know which direction to focus on.

When we do not get what we want in life, it doesn't feel so good. It can even hurt. When we hurt, we in effect whisper to the universe, 'I want more hurt.' The universe is happy to comply. 'Your wish is my command,' it responds.

There really is no point in waiting another minute for the physical manifestation to present itself. If you imagine your dreams came true already, and you are now living in the aftermath, then you will feel the feeling you were searching for. Now you have become a magnet for physical forms that match this feeling.

Before I was living the lifestyle, I'm living now, I imagined it already done. I became the person I imagined myself to be before I even received a single client, the new car, the school for my daughter, the wonderful connections with other families, the income, the body, the close connection with my husband, and all the other wonderful experiences I am joyfully living in the present.

The core of this issue is a revolutionary understanding of what it means to *desire*. The more authentic meaning of desire is found in enjoying something—really wanting it in the sense of relishing it. Desire is a spiritual experience of cherishing someone or something.

Relationships are a good illustration of what desire means. Too often couples really want each other in the sense of craving each other before they get married. Once they marry, before long many of them no longer want each other with the same passion. In most marriages there's far too little desire between partners, so that making love becomes an imposition, not a passion. How many couples have one foot in and one foot out of their commitment?

Desire is generally thought of as an emptiness yearning to be filled. When we are in touch with our essence, we are not at all needy. Our centre is not a vacuum that seeks to suck the world into it. Far from being empty, with little to give, we have infinite resources within us because we are one with the source of everything.

Desire emerges out of a sense of *fullness*. Its wanting to experience the ever-flowing river at our centre, a fullness that has been dammed up for years. This is because at least part of our mojo, if not the whole of it, was stomped on as we grew up. The neediness that results produces the grasping attachment that is a source of heartache. When desire is experienced as a fullness seeking to be expressed, it leads to an ecstatic feeling of fulfilment.

Discovering desire as a fullness that seeks ways to express itself means learning to distinguish what we really want from our whims. How often have we pursued people, things, and experiences we imagined would make our life exciting, only to discover that we were craving something we didn't really want once we got it?

Our true desires emanate from our essential being. Fulfilment at home, work, and play necessitates getting in touch with these desires and bringing them to bear on our daily life. We must become crystal clear about what we want. This is not always easy and takes becoming quiet. We enter stillness and allow ourselves to feel what emerges. When we become aware of what matters to us, we focus our attention on this and allow ourselves to become intentional about inviting it into our lives.

To live is to enjoy, not just endure. Enjoying is what makes life abundant. The most intimate, most 'me' thing about each of us is the form our desire takes—our particular likes and dislikes. One loves to cook, another crafts fine furniture, and yet another paints.

We want what we want because of the person we are and how we want this to expand. When we practice being who we want to become, and we practice this daily, eventually we start to make choices and decisions that someone living a joyful journey through life would make. We start seeing evidence in our life of experiences that bring us joy.

When we imagine something as already done, our subconscious starts to believe that it's *really* done. It does not know the difference between what is real and what we imagine.

EXERCISE

1) Spend the day imagining yourself already in the body you want, with the health you desire, living a wealthy life whether it is wealth in your finances, your business, or a wealth of deep and meaningful friendships. Imagine a life of connections, a life of love. Imagine you are already living a satisfying and fulfilling family life. Imagine you have the qualities you wanted to develop. Imagine yourself being the person you wanted to become.

2) Spend a day acting like you already have it, whatever 'it' is for you. Feel it in your body. Make adjustments around your environment if need be.

3) Release items that don't fit your future vision.

4) Ponder these questions, or better still write down your answers. Start getting crystal clear with who you will be when it's already done.

How will I dress?

How will I behave?

What qualities will I have?

What mood will I be in?

What will I be doing that I'm not doing now?

What will I stop doing that I do now?

What will my environment look like?

Who will I be spending more time with?

How will I spend my day?

Process #17

Unlocking your Intuition

When we evoke inspiration within us by doing processes such as visualisation, thinking about the why, connecting to the essence of what we want, and imagining it already done, we receive ideas, insights, and nudges.

We are talking about our *intuition*. However, many of us mistake a 'gut' feeling for intuition. We get a gut feeling to make a decision or take action.

When the gut feeling feels right, it feels so good that it is an indication to take the action. But beware. A gut feeling can be tainted by the way we have grown up and therefore influenced by our ego.

The same is true of the opposite feeling, which is known as a 'red flag.' A red flag is widely thought to be our inner being guiding us to stay away from a particular course of action. If we experience resistance—if we feel uncomfortable in our gut, or something keeps nagging at us—we are likely to interpret this in terms of 'don't go there.'

Our upbringing programmed us to react in ways that can stop us from growing. If something does not feel familiar, we're likely to resist it.

Based largely on how we have been programmed over the years, or how we have rebelled against our programming and chosen a different mindset, what our gut tells us is *subjective*.

Many of us have done this with dating. We meet someone and are drawn like a magnet by what we call 'chemistry.' The situation ends up disastrously. Or the opposite happens. We begin to feel a resistance within ourselves, tell ourselves it is a red flag, and withdraw from what could be a perfectly wonderful relationship.

On a lighter note, consider the feelings that arise related to a roller coaster. One person experiences the thrill of a lifetime, whereas the other is petrified.

Neither gut feelings nor red flags are divine consciousness. If you look closely at both a gut feeling or red flag, you will see that many of them are *fear* based. With divine consciousness, there is a calm knowing. Consciousness involves no fear. "Perfect love casts out fear," it's been said. Fear is not our barometer of whether a path is right for us. As we have been seeing, often the right path means forging ahead *despite* our fears.

Before I said yes to be my man's wife, my gut feeling was to run and never look back. Friends and family were telling me to listen to my gut feeling. But there was another part of me that propelled me to marry him. There was a knowing that this relationship would bring us both growth. That part of me was not my head, heart, or gut. It was my intuition. I ignored all the red flags because I knew they came from fear and not love. I married my man Nick, and our relationship has been growth, growth, and more growth.

There is a story from two and a half thousand years ago about a man who wanted to see God. He stands on the mountain to which he has journeyed. Then the drama begins. First there is a wind, perhaps a tornado or hurricane, so powerful that it breaks rocks apart. An earthquake follows the windstorm. After the earthquake comes a firestorm, a huge display of lightning. In none of these does this individual recognise the divine, even though humans have long tended to associate God with dramatic events.

Only when the drama is over does the individual perceive the divine presence, which comes in the form of 'a still small voice.' That translation does not quite capture the meaning. Neither is it just 'a gentle whisper; or 'a low whisper,' as some suggest. Instead, the individual hears *'a sound of sheer silence.'*

The expression 'a sound of sheer silence' points to a stillness that is much deeper than anything we can talk ourselves into. It's fundamentally different from an enforced state of emotional peace brought about by disciplining our thinking. It's a bedrock state that's pregnant with divine presence. It takes the form of pure *knowing*.

An intuition is our essence guiding us through a combination of heart and mind. But we must be clear what we mean by these terms. If you try to follow what people generally refer to as your 'head,' you will live with interminable arguments with yourself as you go back and forth on an issue. If you follow what people tend to have in mind when they speak of your 'heart,' you will experience an ongoing stew of emotional turmoil. In both cases, the name of the game will be confusion, anxiety, and *drama*.

When people speak of their head, they tend to imagine being jerked first this way then that by churning and often conflicting thoughts. It is important to recognise that thoughts are just thoughts and don't necessarily represent our analytical powers, our intelligence, our logic. As we noticed in an earlier chapter, many of the thoughts we have are ridiculous. The wise person allows them to come and go without either dwelling on them or fighting them. We accept that they just are, a feature of existence that's common to all humans. Don't worry. If you think really crazy thoughts, so do the rest of us.

Just as our thoughts can lead us down the garden path, so too can our emotions, which aren't at all what real 'heart' is. If you follow only your emotions, you are likely to complicate your life. One minute you will be set on going in a particular direction, whereas the next it's 'all change.' As I mentioned earlier, you can be so in love with someone one minute, but when they do something you don't like, you find yourself yelling, 'I hate you! I never want to see you again.'

Heart isn't simply an awareness that something feels good. It might feel good to be in free fall from a plane, but if you fail to pull the ripcord you are going to end all feeling and all thought. If you have a one-night stand through which you catch an STD, your future enjoyment of sex may well be jeopardised. If you eat junk foods that the bad bacteria in your gut thrive on and cause you to crave, pretty soon you are destined to be ill.

Our intuition gives us tuition from deep inside ourselves, with the 'in' pointing to inside and the 'tuition' pointing to teaching. It teaches us from *inside*, guiding us step by step by means of our deep desires.

When my daughter was ready to eat solids at six months, I had the opportunity to teach her to connect to her intuition as well as to learn healthy eating habits.

I was stubborn about not leaving Ashani with babysitters and not having visitors at her mealtimes because I wanted to use her mealtimes as an opportunity for her to learn to listen to her intuition.

I did this by placing food in front of her at set mealtimes during the day. She was learning how to hold food and chew it by watching me. When her body had enough food, she stopped eating. I cleaned up her highchair, face and hands, and ended the mealtime.

As she grew and learnt to speak, she was able to voice when she had had enough. Even if she did not finish her food, I ended the meal with a smile and moved on to the next activity. You may ask, "How does this teach children to listen to their intuition?"

I could have said things like, 'Finish your veg, and then you can go' or, 'Finish it all. There are starving children in the world.' I could have coaxed, 'Just one more mouthful, then you can stop.' Manipulation, threats, and guilt trips come from fear. Fear of our children going hungry, not eating enough, missing out on vital nutrients.

We love our children and want to be a 'good' mum for them. However, reacting to the instant rush of fear that arises when we see food on their plate and hear the words, 'I'm finished' is denying our children the connection to their own intuition, which they will need in the future if they are to continue growing and evolving when they fly the nest.

Teaching our children to rely on other people's intuition instead of their own can knock their confidence, limit their independence, and develop a fear of making important decisions for their future.

The result of my experiment, which came from my intuition, resulted in my daughter not only having a pallet for vegetables and fruits, along with other healthy eating habits, but also a connection with her intuition.

When I have listened to my intuition, I've always had amazing experiences. My intuition led me to this point in my life and I am forever grateful. When we take action from within, we are co-creating with our true self. I happen to believe we are co-creating with a higher force that is greater than us. This is why our intuition is always right.

When my intuition tells me not to do something, I listen to it. Or if it gives me the 'yes' feeling, I listen to it and take the required action. My essence knows what I need to do to move toward my dreams, and what not to do. Infinite intelligence is far more clever than the ego will ever be. The universe is wiser and smarter than us. When we ignore guidance, the sense that we need to do something or give up doing something becomes stronger until we are forced to act. Some people are so stubborn that they would rather die than open their mind and connect with their inner knowing.

It can be scary at times to take action, and we may even question whether our intuition is truly guiding us. It is okay to seek reassurance. In fact, it is the prudent thing to do. You will be shown the way— and if you ignore that way, you will be shown another way. This will keep going on until you say 'yes.'

I cannot emphasis enough the importance of learning to enter the 'sheer silence' that lies at your centre. This is the key that unlocks our intuition.

EXERCISE

Spend a day connecting to your intuition. Do this without trying too hard or judging yourself if you cannot connect to it straight away. Just like toning up a muscle in the body at the gym takes consistency and many trips to the gym, all the processes I am sharing with you in this book are meant to be practiced as a way of building your mind muscles.

1) Silence your mind by removing distractions and getting into a comfortable, relaxing position.

2) Close your eyes and take as many deep and slow breaths in and out until you can sit still in silence without responding to any thoughts.

3) Ask your intuition for guidance on a situation you require support in.

   Example: 'Give me the best way to teach my baby healthy eating habits.'

   'What do I need to do to start my own business?'

   'Should I move in with my boyfriend?'

You will be able to discern when you are trying to answer your own questions with your ego mind, and when you are receiving an impulse, nudge, or insight from your intuition that leads to an inspired action.

It may come straight away. It may come when you least expect it.

In my own experience, I receive the inspired action from my intuition when I am feeling joyful.

Process #18

Be Inspired

When someone else has what we desire, we have a choice. We can turn into a green-eyed, jealous, bitter woman, or we can look at the individual through eyes of admiration. The choice we make comes from what we believe about ourselves. If we believe we cannot have what they have, our faith is focused on lack and limitation. If we believe it is possible to have what they have, we choose to have faith in abundance.

Lack majors in fear and repels what we want. Abundance majors in love and attracts what we want. Focus on lack activates the jealous and bitter woman that is an aspect of ego. The feeling of love and the focus on abundance activates the confident and joyful woman within us.

Many women give their mojo away in lack and limitation because they see other women having what they want and believe they cannot have it for many reasons. They tell themselves they are not lucky enough, not rich enough, not pretty enough, not clever enough, not supported enough, or there's not enough time. They may think they are too old or too young. All these reasons come from a self-belief that's based in ego, not one's essence.

When you trust your essence, you believe you can achieve a life you love. When you see other people obtaining what you want, you feel happy for them. When you are focused on what you don't have, you are resentful. Supporting and admiring other mums who have what you want keeps you on your path toward your own success. Be inspired by other mums, using this inspiration to compel you into taking action toward your own desires.

Feeling jealous of others is not in line with your mojo and fails to create a life you'll love. Seeing others as a threat or a reason to belittle and beat yourself up gnaws away at your self-esteem and confidence. Being inspired by other successful mothers attracts your own success.

We all have the unlimited potential to be, do, and have anything we desire.

It is said that we become who we spend our time with. Most of the people I socialise with are wealthier than me, more successful than me, healthier than me, more authentic and confident than me. Because I am inspired by them, this gives me a higher level to rise to. I love being in their homes because they live in the type of home that's my heart's desire. I love the feeling of knowing what I can choose if I wish to.

I am so inspired by them and excited about what I have the potential to be, do, and have.

Spending time with people who are judging the choices you make for your children, criticising your choice of clothes or car, making fun of your appearance, telling you what you should and shouldn't do will only make you feel mojo-less. When we feel mojo-less, we become disconnected from our essence and subconsciously start behaving like those people who knocked us off our path.

This is why it's important to be around the kind of people you aspire to become. They will propel you forward toward your heart's desires.

If you want what someone else has, whether it is a passionate love relationship, a family holiday, a stimulating social life, a satisfying and fulfilling family life, or simply inner peace, look at others who have this and say, 'I choose this for myself.' Believe it's possible, and you will create it in your own life. Looking at someone else and saying, 'I wish I had that' won't bring it into your life. If you do receive it, you will not feel fulfilled because of your initial feeling of lack.

Looking at someone else and saying with optimism and gratitude, 'Thank you universe for showing me what's possible. I also choose this.' This feels so good that your body will inspire you to do something positive about it.

Ten years ago, I was living in a town called Reading in England. My husband and I were at the dating stage in our relationship at the time. I was working a full-time office job in I.T. Monday to Friday from 9 a.m. to 5 p.m. One lunchtime on a pay day, I went into town browsing through the clothes shops.

I noticed a fabulous looking woman who was also browsing through the rails of clothes. She was absolutely stunning. I couldn't help but notice the positive vibe she exuded. She looked like she was in her forties, healthy, and wealthy. She had a freedom type of vibe about her, as if she had all the time in the world.

Something inside me made me want to approach her. 'I hope you don't mind, but you are absolutely stunning,' I said straight from my heart. She smiled and said thank you. We got into a conversation.

I told her that she had such a positive free vibe about her and asked her what she did for a living. She said she had her own business in holistic healing. She also shared that she was married with two children, who were both in school.

I was totally inspired by her lifestyle and vibe. I told her how inspired I was. As I walked back to work, I felt so positive and excited about my future. 'When I get married and have kids, I want a life like hers,' I said intentionally to the universe.

It was eight years later, and I was in Birmingham shopping centre, in my own world browsing through the rails in a clothes department. A woman asked me, 'There is something about you, do I know you?" She didn't look familiar to me. I told her I was not from around this area.

She asked me what I did. 'I have my own life coaching business," I told her. She asked me if I was on my lunch break. I explained that my daughter had recently started full time school and I had the rest of the day to myself until it was time to pick her up. "Lucky you" the woman said, and we parted.

Then it dawned on me. 'I'm that woman in Reading!' It became clear to me how I was so uplifted by the woman's lifestyle back in 2010 that my intuition had been guiding me with inspired action steps ever since.

It was this same intuition that told me to say 'yes' to marrying my husband, the same intuition that nudged me to move back to my home city, the same intuition that nudged me into a career change.

Being inspired by others opens you up to inspired action. We only have to focus on what we want and believe we can have it too.

It takes practice to change this habit from feeling like you cannot have something to feeling like you can have it. I still to this day struggle at times to believe in myself. After a little reminder that I can achieve whatever it is I desire, and allowing my self-belief to rise, in no time at all I achieve my dream.

Occasionally, life's challenges can knock my self-belief and confidence. When that happens, I go within, get quiet, staying still, hibernating from the world. I release the disempowering feelings and shift my focus and faith back onto a positive, empowering, joyful note. The processes in this book are great for shifting your focus and faith back to abundance.

When I shifted my focus and mindset and started to achieve my dreams and goals, people who were close started to push me away. Some were simply unkind to me. If this happens to you, trust that whatever is happening is for everyone's good. Stay focused on your faith in abundance. If people cannot be happy for you, do not take it personally and never use it as an excuse to dim your light just to make them happy. Not everyone will be conscious and awake, and not everyone is ready to learn what you are learning right now.

I appreciate what my husband's nanny says, "It's water off a ducks back!" I love that attitude.

EXERCISE

1) Spend a day observing other people but do it discreetly as you don't want to come across as a stalker!

2) Go through magazines, look at the people in the TV programs you watch, and wherever you go be open to noticing what you want for yourself someday.

3) When you see someone, who has what you want, say to yourself, "Thank you universe for showing me what I can have. Yes, I choose that or something better."

4) Choose to feel enthusiastic and excited. See yourself experiencing it in your life.

5) Believe you can have it, that you deserve it, and that you are worthy of it.

Process #19

Celebrate Inspired Action!

CONGRATULATIONS! You have learnt the principle that physically moves you toward your heart's desire. A desire without action is just a desire. A desire with action is a creation of the desire.

The journey we go on to turn that desire into a creation is magical. Congratulate yourself, celebrate big time because you have just learnt some of the best processes that make magic happen.

This principle is called, 'The most joyful journey through life is created by taking inspired action.' The joy is in the journey, not in the destination. The creation of the desire is a symbol of the journey you just went on.

The difference between women who are successful and happy, and women who are stuck in lack and are miserable, is not only their self-belief. It is the action they take. Taking action toward your dreams is vital for creating what you want.

It is action that builds on self-esteem and confidence. It is action that gets it done. The action you choose makes it happen. Action taken through willpower disconnects you from your mojo. Action taken through inspiration connects you to your mojo.

Take a moment to acknowledge and honour yourself for being willing to take inspired action and going for what you deserve. Whether you are doing the processes in your mind or writing them down, it does not matter. Either way is taking action.

You are an amazing role model for your children, who are watching you all the time. They are learning how to set themselves up for success and to create magic in their own lives by watching you take inspired action. Way to go, smart mum!

How do you intend to celebrate yourself today? You deserve a treat—something special that is just for you.

I am celebrating by treating myself to a large jigsaw and maternity tops today for writing up this chapter and for having the courage to share truths that could push buttons for some.

Affirm proudly out loud, 'I am inspired and ready to take action toward my desires, and I believe in myself.' Then go for it!

Chapter Four

R is for Respond

Principle #4

Responding to Life with Acceptance, Love, Appreciation, and Gratitude Is the Gateway to Abundance

This principle will help you cross the line from inner turmoil and chaos to inner peace and harmony. The by-product of inner peace and harmony is abundance. The four attitudes to creating an essence of inner peace and harmony are:

Acceptance

Love

Appreciation

Gratitude.

Responding to life with these four attitudes is the gateway to abundance. An abundance of good health, wealth, and joyful experiences are facets of your mojo. Reacting to ourselves and life's events with rejection, resentment, a lack of appreciation, and ingratitude is the gateway to lack. It will cripple your mojo.

An abundance of health, wealth, prosperity, and joy comes from accepting, loving, appreciating, and being grateful for your health, wealth, and prosperity each and every day. Even if you are forty pounds overweight and have only a penny to your name, this principle stands.

No matter how terrible a situation, first comes acceptance, then love, then appreciation, and last but not least comes gratitude. Whatever situation you are experiencing and do not want to experience, first accept that whatever has happened, has in fact happened. Only after acceptance can you move toward a solution.

If we react to the unwanted situation and stay stuck in 'that shouldn't have happened. Why has it happened?' this is the opposite of acceptance. I know people who can't accept how they have been treated in the past. Ten, twenty, thirty, even forty years later they are still stuck because they aren't willing to accept that someone else behaved in a way they did not like.

I also know people who in the past have lost a lot of money and to this present day talk about the situation with bitterness and resentment. They are stuck in disempowering feelings that can never bring abundance. They only bring more pain and further lack. I understand some situations can be hard to accept. In such cases, I strongly recommend speaking to a therapist, counsellor, or coach. Love yourself enough to find the help you need. It will bring you freedom and inner peace.

Acceptance brings a sense of closure to disempowering feelings about a situation. It immediately shifts the vibe we send out. When I was forty pounds overweight, I had to come to a place of acceptance before feeling any kind of love, appreciation, or gratitude for my health. Until I accepted that I was overweight, I was stuck in not feeling good in my skin and clothes. Once I accepted what I had done to my body and health, my vibe changed from feeling sorry for myself to 'let me do something about this.'

Once we accept ourselves, it is easier to accept others. The need for people to act differently toward us goes away. We can either choose to be stressed out, or we can choose acceptance and move on with life.

When our daughter was diagnosed with a heart defect at age four, my initial reaction was worry and fear. By the end of that day, my husband and I had accepted it. We knew we needed to move out of fear and worry into acceptance, so that we could move forward with a positive attitude. We then moved into an attitude of love.

From that day forward, we responded to all correspondence with the hospital with love. We were able to respond with love to our daughter's meltdowns as a result of the tiredness she felt. We were able to respond to the waiting list for the surgery with love. We were able to focus on our careers, social events, and difficult people too, all with love.

We all have a choice. We can either use a situation to break us or we can use it to make us. We can either shrink, or we can choose to grow. The heart defect experience was an opportunity for the three of us to grow. If we stayed stuck in worry and fear, we would not have been able to enjoy the time together as a family. We would have snapped at each other because our tolerance levels would have been low. We would not have attracted abundance. Instead, we would have experienced lack. Finding acceptance and moving into love resulted in us all sailing through the months it took until the surgery—and a very successful heart surgery it was.

Appreciation is the next step. Once my husband and I accepted the health scare and responded with love, we were able to appreciate that the defect was found. We appreciated the NHS, the doctors, and the nurses. When we were told there was a six-month waiting list, we chose to appreciate that we were in a country where the operation could be performed. We appreciated everyone's time and how sweet and reassuring they all were to our daughter. We only spoke words of appreciation. Instead of choosing to complain about the waiting time or the hospital, the doctors, the nurses, the NHS, or the car park charges, we chose to appreciate it all.

From appreciation, we moved to gratitude. What a high, abundant vibe gratitude is. The feeling of gratitude creates space for abundance to fill it. Whether it's an abundance of love, an abundance of wealth, an abundance of joyful experiences, whenever we truly feel gratitude, we receive abundance. The more grateful we are for our family, the more joyful experiences are created to be grateful for. When I am in a deep feeling of gratitude for my life, my family, and what I have, my daughter feels my energy and comes over to me and snuggles with a content smile. A positive vibe is comforting for our children.

Responding with acceptance, love, appreciation, and gratitude saved my marriage and created an abundance of love and joy in our relationship. Once we accept another person, it is easier to respond to them with love. Acceptance helped me to release my neediness. I feel embarrassed to admit I was needy in my relationships, which is one of the reasons they tended to fall apart. Once I learnt to accept the things I cannot control, and to have faith in abundance instead of fear, things turned around in my marriage.

I quit the complaining, the nagging, the desperate pleas for love, appreciation, and attention. Once I stopped reacting out of fear of spending a lifetime without a love connection with my man, and instead started to respond with love, appreciation, and gratitude, I became happy without needing anything from him. It was amazing. My self-esteem grew, my confidence grew, and I felt on top of the world. My man loved it. The more I appreciate him for providing for our family, the more he wants to provide for us. The more grateful I am for my husband, the more he is grateful for me and our family.

Focussing on what is going wrong and what's not working provokes a disempowering reaction. When we are focussed on lack, we take action that creates even more lack. You will find as I did that peace with your current situation attracts even more peace into your life.

This starts with *you*. When you practice this principle on yourself and respond to yourself with acceptance, love, appreciation, and gratitude, you begin your transformation and start getting your mojo back. Many women are waiting to feel accepted, loved, and appreciated by their partner, their children, their parents, their siblings, their in-laws, their friends, and everyone else before they are willing to respond to themselves with love and appreciation. While they wait, they hurt and are resentful. They feel unwanted, unloved, unappreciated, not good enough, not liked, rejected, and consequently lonely. This is disempowering and undermines their mojo. They end up reacting to people and circumstances with anger, criticism, judgement, and belittling. Or they might become withdrawn and depressed. The longer they wait to change their approach, the more disempowering feelings build up, eventually creating disease in their body.

Before I even acknowledged my insecurities, I needed everyone in my life to make me feel accepted, loved, and appreciated. Marriage and motherhood brought all my insecurities to the surface, which enabled me to tackle them one by one. It took me a while to acknowledge and accept my insecurities. When I did, happiness began to emerge from within.

Seeking reassurance from our partner and others for how we are doing as a wife or partner, and how we are doing as a mum, creates a needy and insecure vibe that pushes people away. The longer I waited, the more weight I manifested on my body. When I decided to let everyone off the hook and took responsibility for my feelings and my life, I started my transformation by responding to myself first with love, appreciation, and gratitude. That is when the weight started to shift.

If you have people in your life who are being unkind, even if you are loving and appreciative of them, it could be because they are not ready to receive your love. This is because they do not have this level of love for themselves. Such love is unfamiliar to them. We can only give and receive love to the level of our own consciousness. The more conscious a person is, the more love they can feel within and without. As you practice this principle and *respond* to people and circumstances rather than *reacting*, you will become aware of conscious and unconscious people. You must remember that when someone is reacting to you, it is about *their* level of awareness.

While you are practicing this principle, especially at first, you may find you are still reacting to people or circumstances. As soon as you become aware that you have reacted, forgive yourself and, if you have the courage, apologise to the person you reacted to.

I used to react internally in the silence of my mind to people and circumstances, then plaster a smile on my face to make it appear nothing bothered me. Once I started to respond genuinely, I felt so much inner peace. I would say I am eighty percent responsive now.

I reacted one Christmas to a family member. Once I acknowledged that I had reacted, I apologised for my reaction. I explained that

I reacted out of fear and was sorry for this. If the situation had happened a few years ago, I would have reacted internally, pretended that I did not care about it, and would have spoken resentfully to a close friend. I would have married the reaction and given my power away. Reacting takes your power away. Responding gives you more power. It is empowering not only to do the right thing, but to be in control of your emotions.

It is a lot easier to respond to people and circumstances when we are feeling great. When things are absolutely fantastic in our life and we are on top of the world, we do not tend to react. We respond more easily. It is challenging to respond with acceptance, love, appreciation, and gratitude when we are around people who are in a disempowering state, especially vibe suckers. Feeling tired, drained, and the like, the life is sucked out of us.

When we allow someone to suck the vibe right out of us, it's easy to blame them for our low vibe. Truth is, we can choose who we are around and for how long we are around them. I understand sometimes it can be difficult to choose not to be around family members because we either love them or they are our in-laws, and we don't want to hurt our man's feelings. In such circumstances, we can deliberately *choose* how much time we want to spend with people.

It's important not to need anyone to be different, accepting them as they are. Accept that it might be a little more work for you to hold onto your vibe. Appreciate what you like or love about them. Find things to be grateful for, especially for yourself and your ability to hold onto your vibe. The challenge is to leave with the same empowering vibe you entered with. Whether it is your spouse, your mother, your in-laws, or your colleagues, it does not matter. Whether your car breaks down, you have a bill to pay, or the breakfast burnt, it does not matter. This principle needs to be practiced in every circumstance.

First there is something important I need to let you know before you go to work with this principle. Verbally accepting a situation, speaking words of love, appreciation, and gratitude, but feeling the opposite within is not going to bring anyone abundance. If you feel pissed off about a situation or a person, and you are feeling resentment, annoyed, or hurt, you send out a disempowering vibe to the universe. You end up creating more disempowering situations.

I thought I was doing right by *acting* loving toward certain people in my life. I believed I was becoming a better person, even though I was feeling hurt and definitely not feeling grateful. I thought by giving to them, along with speaking words of appreciation and gratitude, would open the door to an abundance of good health, wealth, and happiness. The opposite happened. I gained even more weight. My husband and I seemed to be more distant. I started losing clients. Even my social life was disappearing. I could not understand why my world was crumbling around me again.

'Fake it til you make it' does not work. We constantly attract what we are *feeling,* in the true sense of the word feeling. Acting kindly but harbouring resentment doesn't create kindness. It only brings more situations to resent. Acting grateful but feeling ungrateful doesn't bring abundance. It brings more experiences to be ungrateful for.

I believe we are here in this earth school to learn how to love. This is why we keep experiencing the same situations until we learn to respond lovingly. As soon as we change how we feel about a situation, it miraculously goes away. Burdens seem to dissipate, stressful situations are resolved, people who are not aligned with us seem to leave or contact with them becomes less. Sometimes it feels better to love someone from a distance.

If your issue is with your parents, the lesson could be to teach you to appreciate them for bringing you into the world to have a human experience. If it is your siblings, it could be to teach you to accept differences in people. If it is your colleagues, it's possible they are in your life to teach you to be assertive or more resilient. If it is your in-laws, the reason they are in your life is so that you could meet your partner. If your issue is with your partner, the reason for the relationship could be to teach you to love yourself more.

Once you figure out the reason for someone's presence, it is easier to drop all expectations you had for them and accept them just as they are, being grateful for them. When you feel grateful, but you still do not feel good in their company, you can love yourself enough to choose to spend less time with them. Life is too valuable to spend it with someone out of obligation. Once I found the reasons for the people in my life, the resentment toward them disappeared and my husband started taking me out, my daughter was happier, friends contacted me, my business started to take off, my weight continued toward my goal, and wonderful experiences were presented to me.

To this day, when I am faced with someone who is reacting in a negative way toward me, I simply remind myself what the reason is for them to be in my life. As soon as I remember the lesson, I relax into acceptance again, which helps me to not take it personally. 'Water off a ducks back!'

We also have to remember that everyone's mind is set to whatever life has caused it to be. A person's mind can be set to family drama, so they will unconsciously behave in a way that could potentially create drama. If we react to them and fall victim to what they said or did, we have just helped them to create the drama.

If someone's mind is set to manipulate, judge, and criticise, they will unconsciously say or behave in a way that could provoke you into behaving in a way that helps them justify their criticism and judgement. Your job is to accept them as they are--critics, manipulators, and all. When you get to a place it genuinely does not bother you because you understand that their experience has caused them to be this way, it is easier to accept them and send them healing love. You can appreciate yourself for not reacting, as well as for the situation since it gives you an opportunity to be responsive and not reactionary. Be grateful for the gift of growth you encountered. Then don't see them often.

As we change the way we respond, the situation falls out of our experience. You can use this principle to clear debts, release people, clear negative experiences, and to start inviting in an abundance of positive experiences and people.

Love, appreciation, and gratitude are the highest vibes in the universe. Imagine what they would do for your mojo.

Process #20

The Power of Your Essence

When we demand our children do their homework, eat their vegetables, take their bath, and go to bed on time, we have slipped into the ego mind of fear, doubt, and worry. When we come from our essence, we somehow speak the right words at the right time. Our children feel inspired to do their homework and enjoy eating their vegetables without any battles. They look forward to bath time and head to bed feeling content. Does this sound too good to be true? To the ego, none of this makes sense.

I believe the biggest battle we have is between our own ego and our essence. It's easier to be head strong than to be truly open. When someone is interacting with us from their essence, we feel good about ourselves. We feel connected, inspired, have a bounce in our step and a smile on our face. When someone interacts from their ego, it does not feel good. It is disconnected. We walk away feeling disempowered.

We usually spend less time with friends, colleagues, or family who live far, so it is easy to stay in our essence with each other. We are so happy to see each other that the ego becomes quiet. Many families get on better when they live far away from each other. If they are close by, it can be hard to stay in our essence. Before we know it, everyone is having ego-to-ego interactions that never feel good. Trying to prove what a great mum we are, what a great wife we are, what a great human being we are—all of this is *ego*, not our essential self.

The fact is the only person we are trying to impress with how good we are is ourselves. When we practice responding to ourselves with acceptance, love, appreciation, and gratitude, we naturally start to feel good enough and do not need to prove anything to anyone. It is such a freeing feeling.

When my clients first try this approach, they are shocked with how many times they catch themselves thinking and speaking thoughts from ego. If you feel you are in your ego most of the day, don't use this to beat yourself up. Use it to celebrate, because being consciously aware of your behaviour provides an opportunity to become the woman you want to be.

As soon as I become consciously aware of being in my ego, I simply forgive myself without judgment and focus my attention on my blessings. You will know when you are coming from your essence and not your ego when you feel love, appreciation, and gratitude.

When my daughter temporarily slips into her ego, my job is to stay in my essence. If I join her by going into my ego, I have no bar other than fear, doubt, and worry for her to raise herself to. If I stay in my heart, the right words at the right time come through me and I am able to support my daughter through the journey from ego back to essence without power battles or raised voices. We can only support our children to the degree we support ourselves. When we look at a situation from the ego, we struggle to find a solution. When we look at the situations in our life from our essence, the solution comes with ease and grace.

Can you imagine the peace in the world if we could all come from our essence?

EXERCISE

Spend a day connecting to your essence.

1) Check in with yourself. Ask yourself, how am I feeling right now?

2) If you are feeling fear, worry, doubt, or any mojo-less feelings, ask yourself, what am I afraid of?

3) Acknowledge what comes up and thank it for presenting itself to you

4) Imagine the fear is a bubble floating away

5) Take a deep breath and choose to go back to your essence. 'I choose love, appreciation, and gratitude'

6) Take out your journal and make a list of everything you love with all your heart. It could be your children, your partner, your parents, your siblings, your nieces and nephews, your friends, your life experience, your home, or your career

7) Once you are feeling back in your essence again, observe the situation and focus on a solution.

Process #21

The Attitude of Gratitude

If there is one attitude to practice, it's gratitude. The profound effect of feeling grateful is beyond anything I know. It's one thing counting our blessings, but to actually feel grateful transcends figuring how much we have to be grateful for. A simple thank you goes far, but a deep feeling of gratitude goes even further.

Feeling the energy of gratitude really is the key to getting our mojo back and creating a life we genuinely love. Most of us are not conditioned to be grateful. Most of us have been conditioned to complain and play the victim. It takes a conscious discipline to be grateful and to connect to the energy of gratitude until it becomes habitual.

When we are grateful for the small things, the bigger stuff comes to us. When we are genuinely and sincerely grateful for what we have, we naturally receive more. The essence of life lies in the fact that what we give, we receive. This is a giving and receiving universe. If we give hatred, we receive hatred. If we give thanks, we receive thanks.

Waking up and starting the day by connecting to the energy of gratitude sets us up for a wonderful day filled with experience after experience that gives us even more to be thankful for. The day flows and goes well. We experience opportunities and gifts from the universe, smiles and a hello from people. Even strangers passing by smile at us when we are connected to gratitude.

Going to bed connecting to the energy of gratitude gives us a restful night's sleep with a sense of peace and contentment. If we focus on what we do not want most of the day, when our head hits the pillow, the mind goes into crazy thinking about the things we don't want. Whether it's money worries or a person who we are upset with, the mind thinks the same thoughts about such things like a stuck record.

We can't think our problems away by thinking about them, but we can make our problems go away by thinking about what we are grateful for. As we give thanks for more and more in our life, the things we don't want, become less and less. The more grateful we feel, the more space is created for the good and the less space there is for unwanted issues.

Our children feel our energy. When they wake up feeling our gratitude, they feel safe, loved, content, and seem to listen better. The secret to end those morning battles is to wake up and connect to the feeling of gratitude. Then see to your child. Before I practiced waking up and connecting to the energy of gratitude, I was inclined to wake up unconsciously. I predicted how the day was going to go and how I was going to feel. I then connected to a mundane, boring, lifeless feeling. The rest of the day went the same way. I used to say before I became a mum, 'Same crap, different day.' With this attitude, it's no wonder I attracted lots of unwanted situations that left me disempowered.

When I changed my attitude to the attitude of gratitude and started my days saying, 'Thank you for giving me another day with my family,' everything changed for the better. This is when I started to attract abundance effortlessly.

The most important takeaway is that you have to *feel* gratitude in your heart centre, your essence. It is a deep feeling in your core. Saying, 'I am grateful for my family' with no feeling does not bring anything to us. Saying it with feeling, like you really mean it, creates more to be grateful for. The more grateful we are for our health, wealth, and joy, no matter how small something may be right now, life brings us more to be grateful for.

When we are in the middle of a challenging situation, it can be quite hard to think thoughts of gratitude. They trick is to pause, take a breath, and consciously look for something to be grateful for. As busy mothers, we are on the go most of the day and our focus tends to automatically go to what needs to be done. If our mind isn't consumed with tasks and time, it tends to be consumed with issues—whether health issues, money issues, family issues, or work issues. When we are not thinking about our issues, we think about other people's issues, such as our children's issues, spouse's issues, or friend's issues. When there are no issues to consume our mind, we create issues just so we can spend our time thinking and talking about them. Then we wonder what happened to our mojo.

If any of this resonates with you, celebrate. Just being aware of your mindset sets up the kind of behaviour that is a good start to transformation. We are so focussed on tasks, time, or issues that we unconsciously spend the day without pausing and taking stock of what we have.

I asked a client at the start of our coaching relationship to write down ten things she was grateful for, and she struggled to find even one. She had practiced focussing on tasks, time, and issues most of her adult life, and even more so since she became a mum, that when it came to finding what she was grateful for, she had no idea. I asked her powerful questions to shift her focus from lack to abundance. This is not uncommon for someone who has been conditioned to focus on lack rather than on abundance.

It just takes one thing to be grateful for, and the mind starts to look for something else. Before long we have a whole new mindset. Basking in the feelings of gratitude is the magic ingredient in terms of your mojo and creating a satisfying and fulfilling life you absolutely love.

When I first practiced being grateful, from waking up in the morning to going to bed at night, I spent thirty days in a row focusing on gratitude. While washing up, I was grateful for every spoon, fork, and knife. I was grateful for every dish and pan. As I did laundry, I was grateful for every single piece of clothing. As I shopped, I was grateful for every person I passed, every isle, the supermarket, the car park, and everything else I saw.

Doing this process all day and every day becomes the mind's habitual way of thinking. Even now as I type this, in the background my subconscious is saying 'thank you for this process, thank you for this information.'

When I take my daughter to school, I say out loud, 'Look at the sun Ashani, it's lighting up the world. Oh, I am so grateful for the sun.' When I walk her to the school gates and I see the lovely teachers and all the children playing in the playground, I say, 'I am so grateful for this lovely school and all the teachers and all the children.'

We can either let our mind choose what we think about and manage us, or we can consciously choose our thoughts and manage our mind. If we let the mind choose, it's more likely to moan, moan, moan! That would be a terrible vibe from which to create our lives.

Gratitude is a powerful energy that rushes through our bloodstream. When I think about how grateful I am for my daughter, I can literally feel the energy of gratitude rushing through every cell of my body. I feel the emotion of gratitude.

Here are some of the things feeling gratitude will do for you:

Feel empowered

Feel inner peace

Feel enough

Feel abundant

Feel sufficient

Feel happy

Feel joy

Feel compassion

Forgive yourself and others

Create healthy relationships with friends, family, and co-workers

Magnetise more abundance and joyful experiences to be grateful for

Improved health

Improved finances

Improved relationships

Create joyful parenting experiences

Find solutions to problems easily

A relaxed and positive attitude

Easy going

Smile and laugh more

The list is endless.

EXERCISE

Spend a day focusing on what you are grateful for to shift your vibe so you can manifest more into your life to be grateful for:

1) As you go about your day from the moment you open your eyes, silently or out loud be grateful for everything you see, touch, smell, hear, and taste.

If you want to write down your gratitude for faster results, following the steps below will make the process more powerful.

2) Pause, take a slow breath in all the way to your tummy, and slowly exhale

3) On a clean sheet of paper in your journal, list ten things you are grateful for

4) As you think of what you are grateful for, put your hand on your heart and really feel the gratitude.

To do this process for rapid manifestation, do it first thing in the morning, at midday, and last thing before going to bed. The aim of this process is to *feel* gratitude most of the day.

Process #22

Breaking Through Limiting Barriers

As you make the decision to reclaim your mojo back, and as you start to take the action steps necessary for a life that is satisfying and fulfilling, you may find that obstacles and challenges pop up constantly. These can throw you off your path and slow you down from achieving your goals. These are the barriers that kept you from moving forward in the first place. They are only arising from old thoughts, feelings, attitudes, and beliefs. The barriers limit you from an abundance of joy, love, success, and all the good stuff you desire.

Barriers make us feel unsafe. The ego freaks out, and this is absolutely normal. It happened to me a lot when I first started on this journey. It still happens now when I have a new vision for my future, and I start taking action. Many people give up at this stage in their journey because the ego says things like, 'This doesn't work,' and they blame themselves for not being able to manifest the life they want and think there is something wrong with them. Or the ego will tell us, 'This is a load of rubbish' and tries to convince us that it's garbage.

Our current reality is the result of our past thoughts, feelings, attitudes, and beliefs. With consistency and perseverance as we respond to barriers with conscious thoughts, feelings, attitudes and beliefs, our future will eventually emerge. Patience is key while our new reality catches up with our mindset.

If you have practiced empowering thoughts, feelings, attitudes, and beliefs, for a few weeks consistently but nothing seems to have changed in your life, check in with yourself with how you have been feeling. Have you been feeling good while you have been thinking thoughts that make you feel good? This is the first point of manifesting the life you want to live. Your feelings are the first manifestation from your thoughts. It takes time to break down barriers that have been there for years or even decades. Each day you practice responding differently to barriers, you are a day closer to your new reality.

Your reward is having your mojo back. Keep your eyes on this reward. Don't give up. Be stubborn with your mojo. Hold onto it. Don't give it away to obstacles, whether the obstacle is a bill you cannot pay right now, the needle on the scale has not moved for a week, your family are creating drama, or you are in the company of someone who passively insults you or indirectly communicates with you to break you down. Change the way you respond, stay focussed on your dreams, and remember that the obstacle was created from past thoughts, feelings, attitudes, and beliefs.

When an unwanted experience presents itself to you, don't react to it or to any mojo-less thoughts your mind chooses for you. Choose to stay calm and respond with acceptance, love, appreciation, and gratitude because you created it from your past reactions.

A whole new world is on its way with the type of people you want to be around, with the financial experiences you want to have, with the connections with your family you desire, with the fit body you dream of, and everything else you desire. Do yourself a favour, break down barriers with your courage, your burning desire to have a joyful and successful life, and with a new empowering mindset. Set yourself free from a limited life. There is nothing like it. It is your birth right to enjoy yourself while you are here.

Benefits of breaking down the barriers:

Increased self-esteem

Increased self-confidence

Expands your life

Mojo giving

Better health

Improved wealth

Freedom

Joy

Empowering experiences

Positive role model for your children

Sets you up for success

Become stronger minded

Get closer to your dreams

Disempowering experiences become less

Empowering experiences expand

Become more attractive

Better company

Feel safe.

EXERCISE

Spend a day acknowledging and breaking down the barriers you are presented with, so your dreams come to fruition faster:

1) Think about the unwanted situation presented to you

2) Pause, take a slow in-breath, and exhale slowly

3) Don't resist how you feel. Breathe through it. Sit with the feeling and allow it to pass

4) Once the feeling has passed and you are feeling calm again, ask yourself, 'What do I want instead?'

5) Ask yourself, 'How do I want to feel?'

6) Remind yourself that this situation is from my old beliefs. Only good is being created out of this. Everything is working out as it should

7) Take another deep breath in and exhale slowly, reminding yourself, 'All is well, and I am safe'

8) From this safe and empowering state, respond to your obstacles and challenges.

Responding to the challenges and unwanted situations in this way will support you in sailing through anything with ease and grace. It is in this ease and grace that a satisfying and fulfilling family life will naturally emerge.

Process #23

Play a Winner's Game

Imagine that you believe in yourself and in your ability to create a life you love. This belief is not something you try to work up. It springs up naturally within you as you increasingly regain touch with your mojo. You can see your amazing future getting closer and closer. You are feeling and looking great. Life is good. How does it feel to imagine this?

Now imagine you have visitors, and one particular visitor tends to speak without thinking and insults you. You have a choice. You can either react to this person and create tension between you and give your mojo away, or you can choose to hold on to your mojo and not give the insult any attention as you focus on your great life.

I'm not saying this is an easy thing to do. When we first attempt not to play silly mind games, we want to react and put the person in their place. I know it can feel good to be the winner of these silly games, but the truth is that when we consume our mind with disempowering thoughts of resentment or revenge, we are only hurting ourselves and our mojo. *If we choose to fight back, our dreams are not big enough.*

If you have people in your life who passively insult you, criticising and judging you, or they speak to you directly with disdain no matter how much you are doing for them, no matter how respectfully and kindly you speak to them, ask yourself, 'Does this person add value to my life?' If the answer is no, ask yourself, 'Does this person add value to my children's life?'

Dynamics of families are always changing. We bring people into our families who are strangers to the rest of the family. It can take time to form a trusting relationship. When we meet someone, fall in love, and make a commitment, we are bringing a new person into the family. That new person will usually come with grandparents, parents, siblings, friends, and possibly even children of their own. A changing family dynamic can bring many joyful experiences, but it can also bring up many fears and insecurities for the rest of the family as well as for the new couple.

In an ideal world it would be lovely if everyone could simply just get along and have fun together. We are human and all have an ego, which developed to keep us safe when we were young. To the degree that we still have an ego, it's always looking for things that can go wrong. We must learn to tame the ego if we all want to get along.

When someone passively makes fun of me, criticises me, or judges me, I know that they are acting out their fears. I have learnt not to take it personally and to let disempowering words bounce right off my empowering mojo. It took me a while to get to this place of peace, but I can honestly say keep trying, keep practicing the tools I'm giving you, and you too will experience peace and freedom around people who act out their fears. You can respond with grace and not react out of fear.

I was passively insulted at my daughter's sixth birthday. While their mouth was moving and disempowering words were blurting forth, I focused on my breath and kept myself centred and calm, excusing myself politely to another room where I could be around people who add value to my life. I was in control of my ego and gave my daughter the party she deserved. My priority was my daughter because this was her day. I did not pay the person much attention, and I certainly did not pay the insult any attention at all.

When we are focused on our dreams and goals, whether the goal is to give our children a birthday party to remember or to just get through the day, we won't let anything, or anyone undermine our mojo. If we happen to fall, we do not stay down for long. We get back up quickly. We recognise that insecure people play games, whether unconsciously or consciously. They may have no idea what they are really engaging in.

'I am not playing your silly little mind games anymore,' I tell myself as I hold onto my power. The universe responds to our vibe and brings us what matches it. If our vibe is carefree, compassionate, and understanding, and the other person's vibe is insecure, fearful, and resentful, these vibes are not a match.

When you choose to shine bright and someone else opts to dim their light, do not expect them to add value to your life. In fact, it is best not to expect anything at all from them. If they are not giving to themselves, they have nothing to give to you. If they are not aware that they too are a powerful being who can deliberately create a life they love, and instead think they have no power over their lives, your light may be a threat to them, which means they may possibly try to dim your light unconsciously. Compassion and patience are key in responding. Remember, they are acting out their fears—fear of not being good enough, not being worthy, not being successful, not being loved. Whatever their fears, they are not your responsibility. If someone isn't nice to you, don't try to fix them or make them wrong. Just focus on your vibe and your mojo. Trying to fix someone drains your creative energy. Making someone feel they are wrong only adds to the negative energy and leaves you feeling mojo-less.

I am sure I've said plenty of daft things in my life and unconsciously upset or insulted people. We are all human at the end of the day. When we spend our precious time and energy reacting to other people's perceptions of us, their choice of words and behaviours, we end up playing mind games with them. There is no time for this. We are busy getting our mojos back and creating an amazingly satisfying and fulfilling family life.

Reacting is a loser's game. Responding is a winner's game.

Benefits of responding versus reacting to people you feel attacked by:

Increased self-confidence

Increased inner strength

You feel inner peace

You feel free

You feel powerful

You feel in control

Your inner light becomes brighter

EXERCISE

Spend a day focusing your awareness on your reactions and responses. This will give you an indication of who and what you need to practice responding to, instead of reacting.

Steps on how to respond to those you feel attacked by:

1) Take a slow breath in and out

2) Say to yourself in the silence of your mind, 'I'm not playing your silly little games. I am holding onto my mojo.' Or if you are feeling a little upset and do not feel like being polite, you can say to yourself something like, 'I allow you to be an idiot and now I release any need for idiots in my life. I invite emotionally intelligent people into my life.'

3) Politely walk away and go to a mirror in a private place. Look into your eyes, telling yourself, 'I love you and I am so proud of you!'

Process #24

Mojo-Love

When I mention self-love to my clients, I tend to get a roll of the eyes or they seem to want to hurry through the conversation and get to the conversation on how to manifest what they want. It is important to realise that mojo love is another word for self-love.

I totally understand them because I too responded the same way each time a coach, a book, or audio mentioned self-love. I would always skip that part or hurry through it to get to the part that told me how to manifest the body I wanted, the peace I wanted, the close relationships I wanted, the money I wanted, and the dream job I wanted.

Let's begin this chapter by acquainting ourselves with the benefits of mojo love:

You feel so good about yourself

It increases self-esteem big time

It increases self-confidence big time

It feels empowering

It's a brilliant role model for your children

You have more to give to others

It decreases neediness

It increases self-sufficiency

It increases independence

People are nicer to you

The universe rewards you with abundance

You become open to receiving

You feel happier

You become a great vibe to be around

Your vibe becomes more attractive to others.

Many people on this journey of learning to be more deliberate with their life come back to me saying they are struggling to manifest what they want. They try to visualise and imagine what they want, consciously choosing happy thoughts and feelings. They stop bitching about people and focus on their positive aspects. They say they have tried everything but are failing miserably and keep defaulting to feeling unhappy.

When I ask them what they are doing for self-love, they give me a list of lies. Fortunately for them I am a coach who can see through the lies and gently but sternly guide them back to the truth. After applying self-love, or shall we say mojo love, the floodgates open to receiving all they want. I wait patiently for the text, 'It works!' You see, all the good stuff we want is all a by-product of how we treat ourselves. It is all gifts from the universe for being kind to ourselves before we can be kind to anyone else. Mojo love is the cause, and the good stuff is the effect.

When my husband started taking better care of himself with a green smoothie in the mornings, committing to playing football once a week, committing to working out in the gym once a week, eating healthier as well as transforming his thoughts, feelings, attitudes, and beliefs, from disempowering to empowering, his career dramatically shifted for the better. He had more love and affection to give to our daughter and myself. Our relationship was getting better. He became a lot more fun to be around.

As I mentioned earlier in the book, I struggled for years to feel loved. No matter how many friends I had, no matter how many family relationships, no matter how much my man told me he loved me, I felt empty, lonely, and lost. After having my own family, I still felt the same. I did not understand why I felt that way. My life was filled with people from all over the globe, and yet I felt like I did not have anyone.

No matter how much money I made, and how many friends I made wherever I worked, I still felt empty, lonely, and lost. I worked all over the country and spent a lot of time abroad, meeting many people. And still I felt empty. After the excitement and overwhelming feelings of love for my baby started to settle, I went back to feeling that empty, lonely, and lost feeling before my daughter turned one. That was the last straw for me.

I decided I was not going to stop until I found the cause of this universal feeling of emptiness and loneliness that mothers feel. One of the answers to feeling fulfilled, content, joyous, and loving is to love oneself before expecting anyone else to love us. Mojo love is the answer to getting back that connection to the universe we all had when we were born. It's our birth right to feel good and to live in joy.

Bad habits are created from a feeling of lack. Whether it's from focusing on current lack or from expecting lack. Good habits are created from feeling abundant, whether from focussing on current abundance or from expecting abundance. We are the best role model for how to treat us. If we treat ourselves with disrespect, we are giving others permission to treat us with disrespect. We tolerate from others what we tolerate from ourselves. When I treated my body, mind, and soul with neglect, self-harm, or verbal abuse, I tolerated the same level of neglect, harm, or abuse from others.

I ask the question after witnessing an unhappy relationship, "Why does she stay with him if he is so horrible to her?" The answer is that he's most probably not as horrible to her as she is to herself. We tolerate poor treatment from others when we are worse to ourselves than they are to us.

I replaced self-neglect with responding to myself with the loving attention I deserve. I substituted self-harm with self-care. I substituted self-loathing with self-appreciation. I let go of a lot of people in my life because I no longer needed the ones that weren't kind to me. I let them go, and I let in people who treat me the way I treat myself. I stopped tolerating abuse and created boundaries.

My husband recently told me how happy it makes him to see me happy. I make myself happy with mojo love. Our partners respond to us with the love and respect we give to ourselves. They naturally want to provide for us and protect us even more when they can see that the relationship is worth it.

If we are worth self-love, this is exactly what our partners will also feel about us. We become worth the attention, the affection, the respect. It starts with us first. A dependent and needy woman is unattractive and draining to her partner. A woman who takes care of herself and is happy for no reason is a joy to be around. She is incredibly attractive to her partner.

Love begins with us loving all parts of ourselves. We have many selves. For instance, the mum self is just one part of us. We may also have a daughter self, a sister self, a friend self, a wife self. These are all different aspects of who we are.

Self-love means to love all our different aspects. If I were to be loving toward Nicky, I would end up focussing only on loving my ego self and neglecting the mother self, the big sister self, the daughter self, the wife self, the friend self, the daughter-in-law self, the life coach self, and the most important self—my essence, the source of my mojo.

When we feel unappreciated, unloved, and powerless in the presence of another, it will usually be because we have not loved that part of ourselves. If you are with your parents and feel unloved, it could be that the daughter self feels like she is not a good enough daughter. If the daughter self in you is craving love and reassurance, don't wait for anyone outside you to give it. You may end up living your entire life without it if you depend on others to love the different aspects of yourself.

When we take responsibility for our own feelings and tend to our feelings of lack, especially a lack of love, feeding that part of ourselves with love will restore that part of ourselves.

Most people focus on what we are not doing for them, rather than on what we have done or are doing for them. They come across as ungrateful and uncaring. They may even punish us by taking love and attention away from us. This can feel demoralising. A mother needs her energy for her children, especially if they are small and depending on her. She does not need feelings of abandonment and isolation, or feelings of unworthiness and not being good enough. Those feelings only bring more unwanted experiences.

To feel good most of the time, respond to all of your aspects with love, attention, and appreciation. A simple acknowledgment for what a particular aspect of yourself has done for your children, your spouse, your parents, your siblings, your in-laws is where self-love begins. Make lists of all the loving ways your different aspects have treated others and send them love.

The first thing to identify is all the different aspects of yourself. Here is an example of my list.

Mum

Wife

Daughter

Daughter-in-law

Big sister

Sister-in-law

Friend

Life coach.

Make a list of all the good things you have done with a particular aspect of yourself. For example, if on your list you have mum, write down how you have been a great mum:

I am loving, caring, and nurturing

I listen to my child

I am always there for my child

I cook healthy meals for my child

I support my child's mental, emotional, and physical wellbeing

I get my child to school and get my child home peacefully

I am present most of the time with my child

I take my child to lots of places where my child can play and have fun

I organise play dates for my child.

You get the idea. Do the same for each aspect of yourself. It's lovely when others appreciate us. But when we acknowledge and appreciate ourselves, it's much more empowering.

After you have made lists for each aspect of yourself, write that aspect a letter. This is healing for the soul and clears resistance and bad feelings. This process creates inner peace and an abundance of love in your life. In the letter, acknowledge what you have done that is good. Appreciate yourself, tell yourself that you are good enough and worthy of love and abundance. Tell yourself how much you love yourself and that you will always be there for yourself. Thank yourself for playing that role and how well you play that role.

Love starts and ends with *us*. It goes out from us and comes back to us like a boomerang. What we give, we receive. This process restores ourselves and heals damaged relationships. It creates an abundance of love in our life.

EXERCISE

Spend a day focusing on mojo-love. Focus on all the good things about yourself. Following the steps below will be healing for you and your relationships as you restore yourself and begin the journey of self-love:

1) Make a list of all your important selves

2) List all the good ways each part of yourself has played her role

3) Write a letter to the most neglected self, acknowledging and appreciating her.

Process #25

Celebrate Yourself and Responding!

Responding to life with acceptance, love, appreciation, and gratitude, starting with yourself, will open the doors to the abundance waiting for you. I hope you are feeling excited and enthusiastic about what will transpire for you in the days and weeks ahead as you master this principle and practice the processes in this section.

I am so happy and excited for you because I know how powerful this principle is and what the processes will bring to you and your family. I still turn to these processes because they bring so much peace, love, and abundance to me—and they will for you too.

The power of the energy of love, appreciation, and gratitude is life-giving, life-changing, and results in a life that makes us jump out of bed with joy every morning.

How are you celebrating yourself today? Be sure to treat yourself because you and your mojo are worth it and deserve it.

I am celebrating writing up this chapter by taking a lovely walk in the park and connecting with nature while I send you love, appreciation, and gratitude for reading my book.

Say aloud, "I respond to myself and life with so much love, appreciation, and gratitude. I am perfect just as I am."

Chapter Five

T is for Trust

Principle #5

Trust in the Process of Life, and Life Will Process Your Desires and Show You the Way

---

It took me a while to figure out what life was all about, yet alone to trust it. My motto as an adolescent was:

"Life is a bitch"

"Life is hard."

I sent these two disempowering statements out to the universe. It is no wonder that my life seemed hard.

Life is what we say it is. If we say it is hard, we are right. If we say it is great, we are right again. Whichever way we want to look, we are always right. We receive what we ask for. If we say it is hard, we are asking for it to be hard. If we say life is a gift, we are asking for gifts.

Life can be good if we only trust that it can be good for us. Trust can be a big issue for most because of let-downs and setbacks, betrayal and abandonment. Because of other humans' choices and behaviour, we make agreements on whether we want to trust life or not. The level of trust we have for life, for people, for anything really depends on the level of trust we had for our parents and other significant people in our lives when we were infants and made our decisions about life based on the role models we had.

Trust is another word for belief or faith. Many of us witnessed our parents placing their faith in fear, doubt, and worries. We watched them believe in things going wrong for them and in the world. We observed the level of trust they had in us as children, in others, and in their own abilities. It's not their fault. However, to live a joyful, satisfying, and fulfilling life, we must unlearn our faith in fear, doubt, and worry, and instead learn to trust, believe, and have faith in love, joy, and in life itself.

Did your parents always do what they said they would? Did they always speak their truth? Were they honest with what they were thinking, feeling, believing? Did you hear them talking about you when you were not in the same room as them? Did they give you broccoli when you asked for carrots? Did they pick you up at the time they said they would?

Maybe you did not trust their responses. Were they consistent with their love, or did they withdraw love every time you did something they did not approve of? There are a million reasons for the mind to decide you cannot trust people.

Just like life happens for us, it also happened to our parents and caregivers. They tried their best like we do. They made mistakes like we do. With that level of understanding, we can let them off the hook and compassionately forgive them for not being perfect. We can also forgive ourselves for expecting perfection.

Holding onto grudges and blame is not trusting that the universe is on our side and wants to give us what we desire. Holding onto grudges and blame repels a satisfying and fulfilling family life, bringing further disempowering experiences.

Total trust has zero doubt, zero fear, and zero worry. When we allow ourselves to trust fully, that's when magic and miracles happen. That is when healing and transformation occur. It's easier to trust what we can see, touch, hear, taste, and smell than this invisible entity we call "life." I totally get that. This is why it is best to start with something small and build your trust slowly. Like any relationship, it takes time, commitment, and intention. Make it your intention to trust in life and just watch what life does for you. As you build your relationship with life, the trust within yourself will grow too.

Life happens *for* us and not *to* us. Have you ever said in a moment of despair, "Why is this happening to me?" I said this numerous times throughout my life. When we look at situations with trust that it is happening *for* us, it changes everything. We are able to see what the lesson and the gift are. From this we discover how we can do better next time.

When we ask life for something we want to experience, life will start to create a way for us to experience whatever we desire. The path is laid out for us, but we have to step onto that path with trust.

People, money, and things need to circulate. They are energy, and energy is continuously in motion. When people and things have served their purpose for our growth, the relationship is complete. We must learn to let it go and let in the new. This is the process of life.

If there are people or situations in our current reality that do not match the experiences we are asking for, situations will be presented so they can be released out of our lives. This may be scary and uncomfortable when it happens. But with trust and our eyes on the prize, we get through it.

Many of us had our desires rejected when we were little. Whether the desire for an extra scoop of ice cream was rejected or a desire to be an artist was rejected, it does not matter how big or small the desire was. When we were little, we did not understand why these desires were rejected. We took it personally and decided at some point in our life that it's wrong to desire. So many of us in adulthood have much doubt when it comes to getting what we desire.

With this perception, we can now know that if our desires feel good and exciting, and they do not hurt anyone, we can trust them and go for them. When I followed a career path, I knew my dad was proud of, I was not happy. Even though I was earning a great income, I was struggling in my career and felt stressed every single day I went to work. But when I decided to trust my desire to be a life coach, I went for it. I have not felt like I have worked a single day since I pursued my new career.

At first, I doubted my desire to be a coach. There was a big part of me saying it's wrong and not a good career move. Nevertheless, I decided to trust my desire, because the desire gave me goosebumps every time, I thought about being a coach. There was a feeling inside me that felt so good, a silent "knowing" that this was right for me. It was the trust in my desire that created the way to change my profession. I am good at it because I love it.

When we trust our intuition and our hearts desires, saying 'yes' to them, the universe always shows us the way and delivers everything we need to support the desire. When I said 'yes' to a career as a life coach, I received everything I needed, including the right courses, teachers, books, clients, and the finances.

You have already been asking for what you desire naturally through your experience of knowing what you don't want and feeling the desire for what you do want.

As mentioned earlier, when we try to make something happen through willpower, force, struggle, sacrifice, manipulation, drama, or stress, we end up creating the kind of resistance that repels the very outcome we wanted. Instead of trying to make something happen, let it happen. Life knows better than we do. The universe is a lot more intelligent than we are. We just have to take a look at the beauty of nature. There is no way we could even know how the ocean, trees, and flowers were created. *Life* knows how.

Everything we have ever desired has been queueing up for us. Letting go of the how, when, and where, and trusting life to know which path is right for us, opens the way. It is not our job to overthink the details of the journey to the fulfilment of our desires. Our only job is to remove fear, doubt, and worries from our rucksack, replacing them with joy and trust as we start putting one foot in front of the other.

Keep looking forward as you have no time to waste on looking back. The path is never ending. It is an infinite path of little treasures along the way that keeps unfolding the further you go. There is no final destination. As one desire is received, another is birthed.

There is no point in competing with anyone else. It is not a race. Your path is where the joy is. The satisfaction and joy are in the journey, not in the trophy, because of the person we become as we grow. Impatience and yearning for what you want will fade away because you will feel so good along the path as you co-create with the essence of who you are, which is the state of joy.

Trust yourself, trust your desires, and trust life, which will show you the way if you are receptive to it.

Process #26

It's on Its Way

Just like there is a gestation period of nine months from when a baby is conceived to when the baby is born, everything in life has a gestation period. The gestation period is a good thing as it gives us time to prepare for what is on its way and to become clear with our plans and intentions.

Can you imagine conceiving a baby, and immediately the baby pops out? There would be panic, chaos, and nothing prepared for the baby. We would not be mentally prepared. The chances are we would wish we had more time to get at least the basic necessities ready, such as milk, clothes, and nappies.

Everything that we desire, whether material things or feelings of peace, joy, and love, they are on their way. But there is a gestation period to clear space for them. This is how I manifested all the things I needed to make our family's life more comfortable. I got clear about what I needed. I cleared space for it on my front drive, in my wardrobe, in my daughter's toy box, and on the calendar.

I had complete faith and trust that it was on its way. If not, then something better was on its way. I allowed myself to feel excited about receiving it. Voila! In hardly any time at all, once I was crystal clear with my desires, it only took a few weeks to receive everything I needed. There was absolutely no drama. It all came with ease and grace into my life because of the unwavering trust I had that I would receive it or something better.

We must first become crystal clear with what we want. If it is a bike, what type of bike? What colour? If it's a car, what make, and model car do we want? What colour would we like? What features would we like? If it is a family holiday, where would we like to go? How many days or weeks would we like to go for? Where would we like to stay? What would we like to do when we are on holiday?

We must get crystal clear about our desires. If you are wishy washy with what you want, expect to receive a wishy-washy experience.

Many people feel they should not ask for something because they do not want to come across as greedy. It is natural to desire joyful experiences. It does not make us greedy—it makes us human.

Once we are crystal clear with what we desire, the next step is to trust that it's on its way because life loves us, and life wants us to feel joy. One important thing to bear in mind is that we will only receive what is best for our and others' highest good. We must be open to receive, but at the same time be open to receive it in a different form if something is not good for us. Trust that life knows best what is good for you.

If you ask for a family holiday with the intention that you want everyone to have a really great time, but the country you would love to visit is going to experience trouble during the time you planned to be there, expect to receive a holiday somewhere different. If you are trying to manifest something and it is not materialising, trust that something better is on its way.

Making space for something shows our trust that it's on its way. We are showing life that we believe in our desires. This takes me back to September 2006. I was single and had a strong desire to have my own family. I got crystal clear with what I wanted in my future man. I was crystal clear with his qualities, values, personality, and the fact he had to be a family guy. I believed that he would enter my life when the time was right for me. I met him two months later.

I did not go looking for him. There was no chase. In fact, I had forgotten all about the list I had written about my ideal partner and was enjoying life. Nick walked into my life in a way that I could never had thought of. Life knows best.

Always trust the gestation period. Remember, patience is rewarded.

Everything you want is on its way.

EXERCISE

Spend a day pondering everything you desire without limiting yourself. As you think of your desires, do not think of them from a feeling of lack. Think of them from a feeling of excitement and believing that you can have them.

Steps to receiving what you desire:

1) Get crystal clear about your desire

2) Trust yourself, trust your desire, and trust life

3) Make space for what you want

4) Be open to receiving something even better

5) Trust it's on its way.

Process #27

Let Go of Control

The how, when, and who is not for us to control. Just like we had no control over our child's eye colour, hair colour, arms, and legs while the child was developing in our womb, what we want will be created and the steps and path will be shown to us. The problem is people want to do everything their way and not life's way.

We naturally go into control mode the instant we have a desire for something. Do not get me wrong, it is great to have a plan. However, the plan is there to send out a vibe to the universe of commitment and focus. Life will at times override our plan and show us a better way that is designed uniquely for us. If life could talk, she would say, 'Well done for making a plan and going for what you want, but I've got it from here.'

Without trusting life to deliver, we rely on our abilities, strength, and finances. We look at our bank balance and say, 'I can't afford to start my own business.' We look at our body and say, 'I'm not fit enough to run a marathon.' We look at our skill set and say, 'I'm not skilled enough to have that dream job.' This is looking at life through a narrow lens.

The same way we put trust in mother nature to grow our child in our uterus during the nine-month gestation, we need to put that kind of trust in our desires. We will be shown the way through insights, intuition, the right people, the right books. All the necessary resources and people will be shown to us if we are open to receiving guidance and are ready to let go of control.

If our *happiness* depends on the outcome of our desires, *we need it too badly*. We become desperate and consumed with the how, when, and who. We get into control mode and are too needy. All this does is vibe out our lack. When we really need something and are feeling desperate, we end up feeling unhappy even after receiving what we wanted. As soon as we surrender and let go of control, we shift our vibe. A new relaxed and trusting vibe puts us on the right path.

Check in with yourself. Ask yourself, 'What do I really want right now?' Are you feeling disempowered in any way? Are you feeling needy? A needy vibe will only magnetise more need. An excited vibe brings more to be excited for.

Letting go off control will most probably feel uncomfortable at first, especially if you have lived your life trying to control things. Learning to trust takes practice. It is especially a challenge to trust life, since life doesn't speak to us through words. If life could talk, she would say, 'Chill out. I'm creating a plan for you to have everything you desire.'

Letting go off control is one of the most freeing feelings. Talk to mother nature and she will listen. Give all your control over to her because she can handle it.

EXERCISE

Spend a day releasing the control of your desires.

1) Think of your desires.

2) Get into a feeling state of believing that you can receive your desires.

3) Without thinking about the how, when, and where, hand your desires over to life. 'I hand this desire over to life to bring it to me if it's for my highest good.'

4) Enjoy the rest of your day with people and activities that bring you joy. Thinking about the desires that you handed over will create resistance and block the natural flow of these desires.

Process #28

Allow

It is one thing learning how to ask life for what we want and practicing processes to become focussed and aligned with what we want, and it's another thing to allow it into our life.

Most of my clients become stuck at this point. The receiving of love, joy, wealth, and success seems to be a hard thing to do until we identify the reasons behind it, release it, and allow in the goodies that life has to offer us.

Below is a list of common beliefs and attitudes that block people from allowing. In brackets are affirmations to allow you to receive what you want:

I do not want to outdo my parents (It is my duty to do better)

I do not deserve it (I do deserve it)

I am not worthy of it (I am worthy of it)

People will get jealous (I am an inspiration to others)

It will get taken away from me (I have the power
to create more)

Other people knock me off my path (I allow others
to be who they are).

Once we identify which beliefs and fears we use to sabotage
our mojo, we can turn them around and start saying the opposite
to ourselves. First, we must give ourselves permission to allow and
receive. Giving and not receiving is all too familiar to the brain. Once
we make receiving familiar to the brain, we open the floodgates.

It is not okay to give, give, give. When there is an equal energy
of giving and receiving, we feel full. We have the time, energy, and
aliveness we need for our family, especially for our young children.

I have been a mum now for seven years. I know how easy it is to
give ourselves away to our child and feel flat by the end of the day.
We do not have anything to give our spouse, which then leads to
feeling needy for attention. We feel insecure, which leads to a low
self-esteem. We then go to bed for the night with lower self-esteem
than we had when we started the day. We wake up the next day with
an even lower self-esteem, then show up for our children with this
low sense of self-esteem.

Being with our children with a vibe of low self-esteem affects
their vibe. They cannot thrive in an atmosphere of insecurity and
low self-esteem. If we are thriving, then our children will thrive.
This is why it is important for those of us who are mothers to allow
and receive what we deserve. We must not starve ourselves of good
health, wealth, joy, and especially our mojo.

Allowing begins with us. It is time to start giving to yourself
and learning to receive from yourself. Give yourself something nice,

maybe a lovely house plant or a nice bottle of perfume. Receive it like you deserve it by telling yourself that you are worth it. Tell yourself, 'I allow myself to receive my favourite perfume because I am worth it.' If we do not learn how to receive from ourselves, we will not know how to receive from life. Not receiving becomes familiar even though it feels disempowering.

Let us take a look at the above list of some of the most common blocks and detangle them from blocking our mojo. The shift from blocking to allowing is simply a shift in perception.

We Do Not Want to Outdo Our Parents

We love our parents. We care about them. We care about how they feel. We want them to be happy and live the life they want to live. If they want abundance, we want them to have abundance. If they want better health, we want them to have better health. If they want to be happy, we want that for them too.

You now know how to achieve health, wealth, and joy. You can make all your dreams come true. You do the daily work by meditating, visualising, and journaling every day. You take inspired action steps toward your goals. Suddenly you are in better health than your parents, earn more money a day, and feel peace while your parents are feeling lonely or stressed. You are in a loving relationship, whereas your parents are cold to each other. It is natural to want to dim your light because you do not want to hurt your loved ones. It does not feel-good experiencing abundance while they experience lack. Because you have empathy for your parents, you sabotage your success out of guilt.

How can the world evolve if the generations do not evolve? Each generation is supposed to do better than the previous generation. The world would not have evolved like it has if the caveman's kids did not do better than their parents. We would still be writing on slates and cooking our food on campfires.

Our parents want us to do better than they did. They want us to be happy, healthy, and successful. They want this for us because they love us. They do not want us to feel guilt and dim our light. They want their children to shine and do better than they did.

Give yourself permission to do better. When I realised, I was sabotaging my health, relationships, wealth, and success because I did not want to outdo my parents, I gave myself permission to do better. I gave myself permission to allow in more without feeling guilty. The more I allow in, the more I can give to my parents. This is a beautiful reason to allow and receive more. When we do better, our loved ones become inspired to do better for themselves. It is a win-win all round.

We Do Not Deserve It / We Are Not Worth It

This is a common belief that is at the root of our problems. Once these weeds are pulled out, life is truly bliss. Such beliefs are dangerous to our life and also negatively impact our children. Raising children from a self-sense of 'I do not deserve it' inserts that disempowering energy into our children. Such disempowering beliefs do not allow in what we want. If we vibe out that we are undeserving, we attract more that makes us feel undeserving. It is time to shift these limiting beliefs and allow in the good that we deserve.

Every time you receive anything, whether it's a cuddle from your child, a cup of coffee or a gift, say to yourself, 'I deserve this. I am worth it.' When you affirm these empowering beliefs, remember to connect to the feeling of worthiness. You have to *feel* it.

If you struggle to feel worthy, I encourage you to write down a page or two of all the good things you have done in your life. Include such things as cooking your child a healthy meal, giving your spouse a hug, doing an errand for your parents, being a shoulder for a friend, being kind to the shop assistant, and appreciating someone. Once you have reminded yourself of all the good things you have done in your life, try again to feel deserving and worthy.

People Will Get Jealous

When something we desire feels out of reach, feelings of jealousy are triggered. However, when we realise our potential to manifest a life we desire, we look at others through the eyes of inspiration and eagerness.

Jealousy is a feeling of lack. It comes from a lack of self-belief. If people do not believe in themselves and the endless possibilities to achieve their dreams, this is their responsibility, not ours. It is their responsibility to read books like this one. They can talk to people who have what they want and ask, 'How did you create this?' Unfortunately, most people set their beliefs in stone and do not realise that they can change their beliefs and create a life they desire.

I would love a sports convertible Maserati. It is my dream car. I believe one day in the future I will drive one if this is still my desire. I do not want one right now because it's not practical. However, when I see other people driving my dream car, instead of feeling jealous, I get excited and look forward to driving one myself.

A quick and simple process when we are in the vicinity of someone with a jealous energy is to consciously hold on to our power and have compassion for the individual who does not believe in themselves. Send them love and see them in your mind's eye as happy and having everything they want. Remember that what we give, we receive. When we wish others to be happy and successful, we also become happy and successful.

Do not hold back for the sake of a jealous person's feelings. See yourself as an inspiration to them. You are a role model for them. If they see you as a threat instead of an inspiration, it is because they are in pain. Your job is to stay focused on your own self-development and desires.

It Will Get Taken Away from Us

Fear of having our joy snatched away is common. I certainly had this belief myself and kept sabotaging my success. This belief crept up behind me, and everything in my life came crashing down. It was quite frustrating until my life coach worked with me on my beliefs. We identified that I had a belief that I would lose everything. Shifting this belief can be as easy as choosing a different belief.

At one point in my life coaching career, I lost all my clients. I did not even have one client left. At the same time, my hormones were all over the place and I gained weight again. My husband and I suddenly became distant, and everything else felt like it was falling apart.

During this period, I heard myself say, 'I knew it wouldn't last long. I knew my joy would be taken away from me.' What a limiting and sabotaging belief that is. As soon as we are aware of our beliefs, we have the power to shift them to one that brings success.

If we have the power to create success once, we can create it again and again. There is no limit to it. If we lose what we have, we can create it again. Once I was aware that my self-limiting belief blocked the flow of success, I told myself, 'I have the power to create more.' This affirmation felt so powerful and so good to me. Repeating it for a few days got me back on my path and everything in my reality started to shift. The weight started to drop again, my business took off, and my husband and I connected again.

The jealous ones are happier when we fall. They see our falling as our failing, and this makes them feel better about themselves. They do not try to help us back up. They may even be nicer to us when we fall, just to keep us down there. This has certainly been my experience.

I would rather have it all, lose it, and create it again than never experiencing it because of fear. Having self-trust, and trusting in life, gives us the strength to pick ourselves up after a fall. Each time we stand back up, we are stronger, wiser, and more conscious. Falling is not a bad thing. It's a good thing because of who we become.

Can you handle falling? How strong are you to pick yourself back up?

Other People Knock Us Off Our Path

Nobody wants to be bullied, criticised, judged. It's not nice and there is no need for it. We do not want to be controlled. Nobody wants to be emotionally manipulated with mind games. It can damage our self-esteem and knock our confidence. It can cause a negative impact on our health and success, and it can even impact our personal relationship with our loved ones.

Unfortunately, as much as there are kind people in the world, there are also unkind people. We must learn to be emotionally resilient, so we don't let in other people's pain. When people are being unkind, it is because they are in pain. I see them as ill people who need to be restored to wholeness. People who suffer tend to feel joy in causing others to suffer.

Just like we have joyous and kind people in our families, offices, and among our friends, we also have people who are in pain and are unkind. When we realise, they are in pain, it's easier to hold onto our power and remain emotionally undisturbed.

Needing a bully to be kind, or needing an unreliable person to be reliable, does not allow others to be who they choose to be. When we do not allow others to be who they are, we feel resistance and end up in pain. This energy stops the flow of good health, wealth, and success from entering our life. When we focus on people's ill behaviour, we end up inviting disempowering experiences into our life. I know how hard it is to accept hurtful people, especially when they are in our family and we have to be in the same room. It takes practice not to let their pain in.

The way I do this is to prepare my mind before I see them. I do this by imagining myself cocooned by a beautiful white light. I tell myself, 'I am powerful, and I am strong. I want to feel peaceful. I allow them to be who they are.' I remind myself of goals I am going for and stay focussed on my path. By preparing our mind before we see people who are likely to be unkind, we stay centred and hold on to our power.

We need to allow people to be who they want to be without criticising, manipulating, or judging them. This is easier to do when we allow ourselves to be who we want to be without fear of being criticised, manipulated, or judged. When we are feeling disempowered and blame others, we close off our flow to the good. This is resistance. If we want to feel good and attract the good into our life, we have to learn to lessen our resistance. I believe that total freedom is when we have zero resistance.

For most people, freedom is the ultimate essence they want to feel in all areas of their life. For me, freedom is the essence I love and live for. I love feeling free to do what I want, go wherever I want, and to live the way I want. I love the feeling of freedom to spend my day the way I want without limitation. I love the feeling of time freedom, financial freedom, and especially the freedom to be *authentic*.

What feeling do you want to feel? When you live a life you love and are high on life, what is that feeling? How can you allow more of that feeling into your life? Criticising ourselves and others does not get us into an allowing vibe. The energy involved in criticising is constricting and tight on the muscles. It sends out a low-level vibe that is damaging to our mojo.

EXERCISE

Here are four steps to help you protect that beautiful vibe of yours:

1) Ask yourself, 'What belief do I need to release to allow more into my life?'

2) Create an allowing affirmation and repeat it every day with feeling. Example: 'I am safe and open to receive all the good in the universe'

3) Make a list of all the people in your life you want to be nicer to you. Read out each name and say, 'Thank you. I now take back my power and allow you to be who you want to be.' Then cross out their name

4) Every time you pass a mirror, look at yourself and say aloud or in the silence of your mind, 'I deserve the good in the universe.'

Process #29

Detach

Detaching is similar to letting go. Letting go means to release something from our experience, whether it is a material item, an idea, or a person.

More than this, detaching means to let go of the *need* for what we desire. It is great to desire something and to focus on it, but we need to let go of *our needy attachment to the outcome.*

Most often we think the outcome will make us happy. We say, 'When I lose weight, I'll be happy. When I have children of my own, I will be happy. When my husband changes, I will be happy. When my children listen to me, I'll be happy.'

When we think this way, we become needy, which is a disempowering vibe that repels the very thing we want. If we believe we will be happy once our dreams come true, it means we do not feel happy in the present moment. As long as we feel unhappy, we miss all the opportunities, events, and good times that lead us to the things we want. It is a vicious cycle and one that must be broken.

Our beliefs were formed through our five senses, so we tend to think with a narrow mind. We hold onto the idea that the only thing that will make us happy is if someone changes the way we want them to. We desire one particular house on a particular road, and nothing else will do. To be happy, we tell ourselves we want more children. We also think we will be happy when we have more time or when our book is published.

When a person changes, we are happy for a short time. Then we go back to feeling unfulfilled. When we buy that home, we are happy for a short time, then default to feeling unhappy. When we have child number two, three, or four, we are happy, then shortly revert to feeling unfulfilled. The reason for this is because we get so attached to the idea that we will be happy when we have this or that.

Do you remember when your child was little and *really* wanted that toy in the shop? Whether it was a doll or a toy car, your child absolutely had to have it. You wanted to make your child happy, so you bought your sweet child the toy. Your child then told you in a sweet voice, "You're the best Mummy in the world." It was music to your ears. Then a few days later, you found the toy in the bottom of the toy cupboard.

Your child nags you to take them to the park or to their best friend's house, but at the moment it's not realistic. Suddenly they say to you, "I'm not inviting you to my birthday!" I am laughing as I write this because this was our experience with Ashani time and time again.

Isn't this what we do? We get what we want, thinking it will fulfil us. Once the novelty wears off, we default to feeling unfulfilled. To break this cycle, we need to stop waiting to be happy and learn how to be in a state of joy *now*, which is exactly what this book teaches.

When we say that the universe may choose to send us 'something better,' this is a form of detachment. We are not limiting ourselves to one particular thing. By saying 'something better,' we are open to receiving what we want in a different form. Trusting that whatever we receive is for our highest good dissipates our neediness, replacing it with a fulfilling and satisfied feeling.

What if a different form of what you wish for came into your life and made you a hundred times happier? You could never have imagined this different form. What if life could magnetise something even better than what you *thought* you wanted?

My current reality is a hundred times better than what I imagined five years ago. The way everything came into my life was beyond anything I could have imagined. I still have to pinch myself when I take a look at my current life. This is achieved by detachment.

Being detached from the *outcome* of what we want is the key to receiving what we want or something better. Being happy now by doing things that make us feel happy gets us out of our neediness. Having the trust that we will still be happy even if we do not get that house, that man, child number two, or that business deal, clears the resistance that repels what we want and opens us up to a wondrous life full of new and exciting experiences.

I understand that the thought of being happy even if we do not get what we want sounds scary and may even trigger feelings of fear. Detaching does not mean you will have to go without. Detaching means you will receive more than your wildest dreams.

Detaching from the outcome of what we want does not mean we do not take action steps toward what we want. It means we go for what we want *without needing it*.

You may ask, 'What is the point in going for what we want if we don't need it?' There is a difference between the feeling of needing something to be happy and wanting to achieve something out of inspiration. When we practice happiness every day by consciously and deliberately doing things that feel good, we become inspired to take action steps toward our goals.

I am inspired to write this book. I am inspired to be fit and healthy. I am inspired to invite my friends over for a dinner party. I am inspired to create a positive environment for my family to thrive in. The inspiration to have a desire come to fruition comes from feeling happy and joyous.

The key is to stay detached from the outcome by not needing it.

EXERCISE

Spend a day feeling good and detaching from anything you need.

Here are some steps you can follow:

1) Do something that feels good and raises your vibe

2) Become aware of what your desires are

3) Be detached from the outcome

4) Connect to the feeling now that you think this thing will make you feel

5) Be open to receiving it or something even better

6) Take an action step toward your desire.

To raise your vibe, do things that make you feel happy now. What you want or something even better will come to you in ways you cannot imagine.

Process #30

Believe in Your Mojo

When we believe in ourselves, we can believe in others, especially our children. When we believe in ourselves and in our future, our outlook on life is positive and the vibe we extend out is confident, optimistic, vibrant, and we have positive expectations. These qualities contribute to a beautiful and positive demeanour that is attractive.

When we send out a vibe of self-belief, we draw to us more people who believe in us, magnetising opportunities to be successful in whatever we want to be, do, or have.

Believing in ourselves builds self-confidence and a healthy self-esteem. A lack of self-belief breaks our confidence and lowers our self-esteem, rendering us insecure and dependent. We are nicer women when we have a healthy self-belief.

When I was a child, my dad believed in my abilities and that I could achieve anything I put my mind to. He believed I could be a doctor, a dentist, a lawyer. He believed in me because he believed in himself. I personally did not want to pursue a career in any of my dad's ideas for me. I had my own mind and knew at my core that art, writing, and mindset stuff were my passion.

As I grew up, I believed in myself and still do. Because I believe in myself, I believe in my daughter's ability to achieve anything she puts her mind to. My dad used to tell me, "You can do it, Nicky. You can do anything you put your mind to." I tell my daughter the same thing.

Because of my dad's belief when I was young, I am deeply grateful. I am a successful life coach, writer, and surround myself in beautiful colours and art that make me happy. I also understand that not everyone's parents had such a belief in them. For some, their parents did not believe in them at all.

Take a closer look at your childhood. If you did not have any parent rooting for you, cheering you on, believing in you, did you have a sibling who believed in you? Or maybe a friend or teacher? Look deeper. Was it an aunt or uncle that believed in you? Who saw something in you that you could not see in yourself?

Believe in the potential this person saw in you. Believe in the gift they saw in you. Believe in the standard they saw in you. How does it feel knowing someone believed in you? Use their belief in you to be inspired to start up that business you have always wanted to start, to write that book you always wanted to write, or to run that marathon you always wanted to run. Whatever you would love to pursue, connect to the belief someone had in you and make it your own.

We must start to think, feel, and talk like a self-believer. So many of us affirm disempowering statements such as:

I am not smart enough to…

I am not brave enough to…

I am not good at…

I am not attractive enough to…

I cannot do that because…

I am not confident enough to…

If we speak from such lack, how can we achieve the things we want in life? Instead, tell yourself the following:

- If I put my mind to it, I can achieve it

- I can do it

- I will give it my best shot

- I can only do my best

- If I fall flat on my face, I will just get back up and try again.

Before every school play or event my daughter takes part in, I ask her, 'How do you feel about doing your play in front of lots of people?'

She replies, 'Nervous.'

When I remind her that she can only do her best, she immediately shifts from nervous to feeling relief. Each of us can only do our best. We cannot do better than our best. I remind my daughter that her best is good enough.

If we adopt this attitude, our self-belief will grow. It does not grow full blown in one go. It takes practice. It takes one project at a time, one goal at a time, one desire at a time. As we think, feel, and speak like a self-believer and go for our desires, our self-confidence grows. As we believe in ourselves, people will appear who also believe in us.

When I decided to become a life coach and a writer, the people who believed in me before did not believe in me anymore. No encouraging or supportive words were said. It hit me hard. I either received a roll of the eyes, no response, and even had a member of my family leave the room when I talked about my new dream. I felt like I could not move off my sofa to take action toward my goals.

Over the past six years, I have had to learn how to tap into the self-belief that my dad had in me when I was a kid. Each time I took an action step, I was successful for a week. Then I'd fall flat on my face and stay down for a month. It was a slow process because I was depending on a belief outside myself. The self in self-belief says it all. It must come from the *self*. Self-belief, self-confidence, self-esteem—*they all come from the self,* not from others. The only person we need to turn to for belief in our dreams of a satisfying and fulfilling life is ourselves.

My husband believed in me from the start, but I was focussed on the lack of support from other people in my life. This was a classic fail. Focussing on what we do not want brings us more of what we do not want. It took a lot of practice for me to remind myself to focus on the people who were supporting me. The more I focussed on the people who were believing in me, and the more I affirmed self-believing statements, my self-belief grew. Overnight, I found I could write for weeks at a time. As my self-belief grew, this book grew, all from building my self-belief.

When we depend on others to believe in us, it takes a long time to make our dreams come true. For you to get your mojo back and create a successful life for yourself, you must *believe in yourself* and in the importance of having your mojo back.

It is nice to have others believe in us, but do not depend on it because they have their own success and joy to focus on. It is tiring for others to put their focus on us and to cheer us on along our entire journey. Letting them off the hook and being responsible for our own self-belief, success, and a joyful life is so much more empowering.

When we feel like we have lost our mojo, lost our aliveness, and that happy-go-lucky girl we once were has disappeared, trying to be successful and create a joyful life is painful, if not impossible. We need our mojo back to feel good. It makes our children sad when we are in emotional or physical pain. They are happy when we are emotionally and physically happy. Our children thrive when their parents are happy and thriving. If we do not believe in ourselves, it doesn't matter how much others believe in us.

With all the self-belief I have now, I believe in you. You can go for your dreams, whatever they are. Remember, self-belief comes from the *self.*

EXERCISE

Steps to build self-belief so you can trust in your abilities to live a satisfying and fulfilling life:

1) Grab your journal and make a list of everything you have ever achieved

2) Write down what you must have believed to achieve what you have so far

3) Repeat this affirmation again and again until you believe it: 'I believe in myself. I trust myself. I can achieve anything I put my mind to.'

Affirmations work best first thing in the morning and last thing at night when the body is completely relaxed, and the brain has slowed right down.

Saying your affirmations without any feeling will not work. Affirmations need to be fuelled with feeling and energy if they are to become a subconscious belief.

Process #31

Celebrate Your Life!

CONGRATULATIONS! You did it. You have taken a big leap into a bright, joyous, successful, and empowering future. Let's do a quick check in. How do you feel about yourself? Do you feel proud of yourself?

I encourage you to pick the processes which you enjoyed doing and continue to do them daily. I have shared many processes with you. However, you do not have to do any that you didn't enjoy doing. The purpose of your journey is joy. You can even find a process to do from this book according to how you want to feel on a particular day.

Take a moment to really acknowledge yourself and all the steps you have practiced reclaiming your mojo to create a satisfying and fulfilling family life. Not everyone has the courage to take responsibility for their joy, to go within, and to go for what they want. You are a smart mum!

How do you intend to celebrate yourself for getting to the finishing line by completing this book? Make it a good celebration. You deserve it.

Being a parent whether you are a mum, or a dad is not as easy as a walk in the park. I believe it is a beautiful journey of personal growth and self-development. We learn lesson after lesson on how to maintain that special unconditional love for our babies. If we are willing to go within, we learn unconditional love for ourselves too. Your willingness to be the smart mum that you were born to be is something to be celebrated.

Say out loud proudly, "I now release any limiting beliefs that shrink or dim me. I permit myself to shine bright with confidence. I trust in life because life loves me!" Life absolutely loves us and wants to give us everything we desire so we can live the successful and joyful life we were destined to live.

I totally and completely believe in you! Now go and make your dreams come true, my friend.

What next?

Book a one-to-one life transforming session with the author Nicky Tegg. Listen to guided meditations, download or join live courses, or attend workshops. Visit www.nickytegg.com

Download a life transforming six-week online program *Magnetise your Dream Lifestyle* with discount CODE: SMARTMUM at www.nickytegg.com/courses/magnetiseyourdreamlifestyle

Join our Smart Mum community and connect with likeminded women from all around the globe in a private and friendly Facebook room: www.facebook.com/groups/smartmum

About The Author

As an expert in the field of personal development, professional life coach Nicky Tegg has enabled hundreds of clients to transform their lives all around the globe through one-to-one personal coaching, workshops, online programs, and speaking engagements. As a result of working with Nicky, clients are freed from emotional agony and go on to create their dream lifestyle with grace and ease.

The link between people's mindset and their behaviour became of interest to Nicky when she started studying self-development as a young teenager thirty years ago. It was after she married her husband Nick and became a mum to her daughter Ashani that she realised most women she knew were not happy. That was when she decided to go full-time into the world of personal development, becoming a qualified life coach so she could support people from all walks of life as they take the driver's seat in their lives.

Nicky's 5 principles can work for anyone. *Be a Smart mum Not a Good mum* brings Nicky's insights to a wider audience for the first time. Her intention is that every woman who reads this book should experience a positive and powerful impact from her words.

You can write to Nicky to share your thoughts about this book at support@nickytegg.com

Printed in the United States
By Bookmasters